EU MARKS A QUARTER OF A CENTURY

EU MARKS A QUARTER OF A CENTURY

Flip PETILLION
(ed.)

INTERSENTIA

Cambridge – Antwerp – Chicago

Intersentia Ltd
8 Wellington Mews | Wellington Street
Cambridge | CB1 1HW | United Kingdom
Tel.: +44 1223 736 170
Email: mail@intersentia.co.uk
www.intersentia.com | www.intersentia.co.uk

Distribution for the UK and the rest of the world (incl. Eastern Europe):
NBN International
1 Deltic Avenue, Rooksley
Milton Keynes MK13 8LD
United Kingdom
Tel.: +44 1752 202 301 | Fax: +44 1752 202 331
Email: orders@nbninternational.com

Distribution for Europe:
Lefebvre Sarrut Belgium NV
Hoogstraat 139/6
1000 Brussels
Belgium
Tel.: +32 3 680 15 50 | Fax: +32 3 658 71 21
Email: mail@intersentia.be

Distribution for the USA and Canada:
Independent Publishers Group
Order Department
814 North Franklin Street
Chicago, IL60610
USA
Tel.: +1 800 888 4741 (toll free) | Fax: +1312 337 5985
Email: orders@ipgbook.com

EU Marks a Quarter of a Century

ISBN 978-1-83970-244-0
D/2022/7849/65
NUR 827

British Library Cataloguing in Publication Data. A catalogue record for this book is available from the British Library.

This book serves as an information resource only and does not purport to provide legal advice. It should not be used as a substitute for consultation with competent counsel. We recommend that you consult with an attorney licensed to practice in a particular EU country regarding your legal affairs and individual circumstances.

We cannot guarantee the accuracy, completeness, or up-to-dateness of any of the information presented in these pages, despite our most concerted efforts in this regard.

The Internet is a transient medium. Thus, references to websites are subject to change without notice. Readers are encouraged to check the websites for current information.

Brands, product names, trademarks, and service marks that appear in these pages are the property of their respective owners and are used solely in reference to the companies' goods and services. Mention of any products or services in this book should not be construed as an endorsement.

This edition inevitably contains errors, omissions, and confusions, which will require correction, clarification and further development in future editions, to keep pace with the ongoing developments in the field. Corrections, comments and questions are encouraged, by email to fpetillion@petillion.law.

CONTENTS

ABOUT THE EDITOR

Flip Petillion is a leading domestic and international dispute resolution counsel and arbitrator. Over more than thirty years, Flip has built an outstanding reputation through his special focus on intellectual property rights, information technology, the Internet, communication and media. During his career, he witnessed first-hand the growing importance of intellectual assets for local and multinational clients. He observed the increasing harmonisation of intellectual property rights within the European Union. These developments led Flip to specialise in a wide array of intellectual property and related rights, including trade marks, copyrights, patents, designs, trade names, company names, domains, domain names, trade secrets and unfair competition. He has handled landmark intellectual property cases up to the European Court of Justice and has been at the forefront of Internet-related matters since the mid-1990s.

While he is particularly known for his endeavours on the contentious and enforcement side of intellectual property disputes, Flip also assists clients in relation to licensing and other IP-related contracts, advertising clearance, IP-driven transactions and strategic advice. Through a global clientele and positions within various important European and international organisations, such as ICC, ICDR (AAA), INTA, Marques, ECTA and ICANN, he has developed an extensive international practice and network. Flip also has an important background in alternative dispute resolution, having served as arbitrator, panellist and counsel in arbitration proceedings administrated by various international institutions. Many of his appointments were directly related to his expertise in the field of intellectual property and new technologies.

Flip regularly publishes on various topics related to intellectual property. He lectures at the Benelux BBMM Professional Education Program for Trademark and Design Attorneys, at the IP and ICT Masters program at Leuven University, and at the EUIPO Trade Mark and Design Education Programme. Flip is the editor of a yearly legal publication commenting significant IP case law. In 2018, he edited a book on the enforcement of intellectual property rights in Belgium, which involved the collaboration of 25 peers. In 2019, he edited a book on the enforcement of intellectual property rights in Europe, which involved the collaboration of peers from all European Member States. He is a frequent speaker at professional and academic conferences and has published several articles relating to intellectual property and (alternative) dispute resolution.

After a decade of partnership in an international law firm, Flip established his own firm in the Autumn of 2017. PETILLION is an independent boutique firm focusing on national and international commercial dispute resolution and intellectual property. The firm provides a full array of international and domestic intellectual property legal services and acts before Belgian courts and before the European Court of Justice and the European General Court. With PETILLION, Flip is pursuing his vision of an independent firm, focused on efficiency and providing client-minded and effective solutions.

ABOUT THE AUTHORS AND CONTRIBUTING FIRMS

(in alphabetical order)

Ana-Maria Baciu, Managing Partner at Simion & Baciu, head of Intellectual Property, Consumer Protection & Advertising, Life Sciences and Dispute Resolution practices, is a regulatory and intellectual property lawyer with more than 20 years of experience, assisting clients in various industries, including retail, FMCG, gambling, IT, e-commerce and life-sciences. Licensed as a European trademark and design attorney, Ana-Maria is advising clients on the full spectrum of intellectual property aspects, both contentious, such as disputes over the validity of intellectual property rights, trade mark / design / patent infringement claims or plagiarism, and advisory work, such as re-branding strategies, transactions, IP rights transfers, licensing or franchising, advice on IP portfolio management and complex IP due diligence, as well as registration / filing / prosecution strategies and anti-counterfeiting work.

Andreea Bende, Partner at Simion&Baciu, head of the Trademark & Designs Practice at SIMION & BACIU in Romania, has over 12 years of experience in the intellectual property field, assisting both Romanian and foreign companies with administration, prosecution and contentious matters in respect of their trademarks, designs, domain names portfolios, as well as copyright and related rights. Andreea's professional experience focuses on intellectual property rights administration, prosecution and contentious matters, in various industries such as pharmaceuticals, tobacco, FMCG, automotive, fashion, media and telecommunications. Over the years, she has advised clients in complex projects, including domain name and copyright dispute resolution, unfair competition litigation, worldwide re-branding simultaneously performed in over 60 jurisdictions, applications for action before the Romanian National Customs Authority, as well as IP due diligence and IP transactional projects.

SIMION & BACIU unites a team of seasoned attorneys and counsellors, with the drive and passion to deliver the best and most helpful results for its clients. With more than 20 years of experience, spanning over several complementary areas of law, our team offers a fresh, business-oriented approach and successfully assists clients time and again. The firm focuses primarily on the following areas of law: Intellectual Property, Gaming & Gambling, Consumer protection & Advertising, Life sciences, Data Privacy and Personal Data Processing, Corporate, M&A, Technology&Media and Dispute Resolution.

*

Alexander Schnider is a co-founding partner at GEISTWERT in Austria. For more than 20 years, Alexander has been focusing on intellectual property litigation with an emphasis on trademarks. His practice primarily involves IP litigation, both at national and EUIPO level, as well as IP transactions in a variety of industries, including interactive entertainment, media, software development, automotive, pharma, technology, and foodstuff/beverages. Alexander also provides IP strategy and portfolio management services and assists clients in monetizing their IP assets.

GEISTWERT comprises five partners whose shared interest in intellectual property brought them together. As experienced and recognized experts in the area of intangible rights and related fields, we founded GEISTWERT, a centre of expertise. This law firm is able to work with a high concentration of a rare type of specialized knowledge, allowing it to keep a close watch on the everyday changes showing up on the radar in the highly volatile area of intellectual property. As a veritable intellectual powerhouse, our main mission is to help clients and colleagues reach their goals in the best possible way.

Based on experience of up to twenty years in some of Vienna's renowned law firms, we can claim, quite immodestly, to be the best of the best. We were able to specialize and to become recognized IP and IT legal experts already early on in our careers. Having reached this point, the next logical step was to create our own competence centre.

Our 'post-material' age brings new challenges. The information society, globalization, the Internet, information technology, the brand orientation of companies, technical innovations and their patent protection, as well as the ever-greater economical stake of the creative industries, are some of the main issues of social change today. The increasing legal regulation of these innovation drivers is something that is being promoted worldwide. The pace at which changes are taking place in these closely interlocking fields has triggered political debates. As a consequence, the legal situation is constantly changing, and the judicial system is subject to growing complexity and fluctuations. The result is a high degree of uncertainty when it comes to legal matters.

Against this backdrop we seek to position ourselves as a competence centre that has a clear view of all the legal developments in the IP world, while constantly following the latest developments in information. Our mission is to support clients and colleagues in all matters related to IP and technology by offering the very best expertise. This, in short, is the value that GEISTWERT promises to provide.

*

Claus Barrett Christiansen and **Maria Rose Kristensen** are IP lawyers at Bech-Bruun Law Firm in Denmark. Claus has 25 years of experience in advising both national and international clients on all aspects of trademark rights, domain names, design right, copyright and marketing law. Claus has conducted a vast number of cases before the Danish Maritime and Commercial High Court, the Danish High Court and Supreme Court as well as the Court of Justice of the European Union.

Maria is a specialist within the field of trademark and design strategy and enforcement. She represents major Danish and international corporations across a wide range of industries, including fashion, furniture, retail and consumer electronics.

BECH BRUUN is a full-service law firm serving a large range of operators in the Danish corporate sector, the Danish public sector as well as international corporations by way of its wide range of products and services. Numbering more than 500 experienced and highly specialised employees, Bech-Bruun ranks among the leading law firms in Denmark.

Bech-Bruun has in-depth experience across several key industry sectors and offers legal services within 13 practice groups having their own areas of expertise. Bech-Bruun also has a strong international focus and has, over many years, built a unique global network of leading law firms for cross-border legal assistance. Bech-Bruun's Chinese desk enables the firm to act for numerous Chinese clients in the Nordic markets and numerous Danish corporations in the Chinese market.

*

Diégo Noesen is a senior dispute resolution lawyer at PETILLION in Belgium. For just over a decade, he has been focusing on European and domestic litigation with an emphasis on intellectual property. Diégo's practice primarily involves complex civil litigation, both at national and European level, in a variety of industries, including automotive, fashion, media & entertainment, technology and telecommunications. Diégo also provides transactional advice and assists clients in protecting, managing and enforcing their intellectual property rights. He has a particular expertise in brand and copyright protection, and domain names.

PETILLION is an independent law firm with a focus on dispute resolution. PETILLION's multi-lingual team helps clients prevent, settle and to resolve commercial disputes through compliance counselling, contract drafting, negotiation, court litigation, arbitration or other forms of alternative dispute resolution (ADR).

Most of the disputes involve court litigation before national civil, commercial and administrative courts, before European courts and administrative bodies, in ad hoc arbitrations, and before leading national and international arbitration institutions around the world, such as the ICC (Paris, France), the ICDR (AAA) (New York, U.S.A.), the WIPO (Geneva, Switzerland), the FORUM (Minneapolis, U.S.A.), the CAC (Prague, Czech Republic), and the CEPANI (Brussels, Belgium).

PETILLION has a particular experience in specific sectors or industries such as Intellectual Property, Information Technology, Media & Entertainment, the Internet, and Fashion. The firm has also worked extensively on matters related to Postal, Telecoms, Energy, Construction and Real Estate, Automotive, Aviation and Aerospace, and Distribution.

*

Gerard Kelly is a commercial litigation partner, practising mainly in the area of intellectual property Law and is head of the Mason Hayes & Curran LLP Intellectual Property team.

Gerard advises clients on intellectual property disputes, including substantial patent litigation and passing off, trade mark, copyright and design right litigation. He has been involved in many of the highest profile IP litigation cases in recent years in the Irish Commercial Court, Court of Appeal and the Supreme Court. Gerard also advises on a broad range of non-contentious intellectual property matters including brand protection, contractual/licensing arrangements and regulatory issues. Gerard is a registered trade mark agent in Ireland and a European Trade Mark and Design Attorney.

Jane Bourke is a senior associate in the Mason Hayes & Curran LLP Intellectual Property team. She is an experienced contentious and non-contentious intellectual property solicitor. She has acted for clients in large cross-jurisdictional commercial court cases, obtaining website blocking injunctions, and disputes regarding passing off and copyright infringement. Jane is a qualified Irish and European trade mark agent.

MASON HAYES & CURRAN LLP is a business law firm with 95 partners and offices in Dublin, London, New York and San Francisco. As legal and regulatory responsibilities become more complex, progressive organisations need the right advice to help realise their ambitions. The expertise Mason Hayes & Curran LLP brings is rooted in unrivalled knowledge of the sectors in which its clients operate, so advice is always set in its commercial context.

*

Jan Peter Heidenreich is a German lawyer with more than 15 years' experience, advising and representing clients in all areas of intellectual property (particularly trademarks and designs), as well as unfair competition, distribution and licencing law. He has extensive experience in trademark prosecution and trademark, design, copyright and unfair competition infringement proceedings, regularly representing clients before district and appeals courts all over Germany. Jan Peter also provides advice regarding product designs, as well as all matters pertaining to cosmetics law and advertising for cosmetic products. He regularly publishes on various IP and antitrust matters and is a regular lecturer in seminars on cosmetics law.

PREU BOHLIG is an independent IP law firm with offices in Munich, Hamburg, Berlin, Düsseldorf, and Paris. PREU BOHLIG's team of more than 30 highly specialised lawyers provides legal advice to international corporations, small and medium sized companies and start-ups. The main focus is on patent, trademark and design law as well as on unfair competition and trade secret protection. PREU BOHLIG's lawyers advise on and act in infringement litigation, parallel invalidity proceedings and in product piracy matters. They also advise and represent clients in the fields of German and European pharmaceutical, medical device, cosmetics and food supplements law.

Eva Lachmannová is a partner at the IP boutique Šindelka & Lachmannová in the Czech Republic. In her practice, Eva has been assisting clients in the prosecution and enforcement of intellectual property, in particular trademarks, designs and patents, for clients in various industries, including automotive, machinery, telecommunications & media or in the pharmaceutical industry.

Šindelka & Lachmannová is a boutique law firm focused on the enforcement and prosecution of intellectual property (trademark, designs, patents, domain names, copyright), IT law, pharma law and unfair competition.

Members of the firm have provided assistance in complex intellectual property enforcement matters both in and outside courts for leading companies in the fashion, media, automotive or tobacco industries. The firm has significant experience in anticounterfeiting matters, representing several premium luxury fashion brands. The firm has also been regularly assisting clients in domain matters both in courts and in alternative dispute resolution (ADR).

The firm's diverse client portfolio ranges from multinational corporations to innovative Czech small and medium-sized companies.

*

Matthew Harris is joint managing partner and co-head of the IP and IT litigation team at Waterfront Solicitors. He has nearly 30 years' experience of English intellectual property litigation, having previously been the head of Intellectual Property and Information Technology dispute resolution at a top ten London based international law firm, before joining Waterfront Solicitors in December 2008.

Matthew undertakes a wide range of intellectual property and information technology work but specialises in IP litigation, advising and acting for clients that range from SMEs to large multi-national companies. He has overseen numerous copyright, design right, trade mark, passing off and patent infringement claims in the English and (prior to Brexit!) the EU courts. He is also an internationally recognised expert in domain name law.

For a number of years Matthew has sat on the English Law Society's Intellectual Property Law Committee, where he has been involved in the drafting of the English solicitors profession's submissions in respect of proposed changes to intellectual property law, both at national and international level. This included giving oral evidence on behalf of the profession to the House of Lords that helped lead to recent statutory changes to UK unjustified threats law.

WATERFRONT SOLICITORS LLP is a highly successful niche Intellectual Property and Information Technology law firm located in London. The firm was set up in 2002 to provide an alternative option to businesses looking for legal advice in a structure that enabled it to cater effectively for clients both great and small. Since then, it has steadily grown in size and now provides advice across a number of different areas of law. However, it still retains an intellectual property and technology sector focus. It also continues to act for the full spectrum of business clients, including individual entrepreneurs, SMEs and multinational corporations, including companies listed on the London Stock Exchange, the AIM and the NASDAQ, and government agencies.

A particular strength of the firm is the conduct of English intellectual property litigation, with cases regularly undertaken for clients in the various intellectual property courts and lists of the English High Court, including IPEC.

*

Paul Micallef Grimaud is a Partner at Ganado Advocates and heads the firm's intellectual property, TMT and data protection practice group. Paul's focus is dedicated to counselling and assisting clients in the media, technology and entertainment area on the legal aspects of their operations. As a warranted advocate, Paul regularly represents his clients in arbitration and litigation proceedings relating to intellectual property infringements, anti-counterfeit measures, trade mark and design oppositions, telecoms regulatory matters, media, slander and freedom of information disputes, data protection breaches and unfair competition cases.

Nikolai Lubrano is an Associate within Ganado Advocates' Intellectual Property, TMT and data protection practice group. He assists the firm's clients in matters relating to IP and brand protection, as well as compliance with their data protection obligations. Nikolai is a warranted advocate and represents clients before Maltese courts.

GANADO ADVOCATES has a long heritage. Founded originally in Valletta – Malta's capital city – the firm traces its roots back to the early 1900s. Today, it is one of Malta's foremost law practices and is consistently rated as a top tier firm by leading rating agencies and legal directories.

Ganado Advocates seeks to provide high standards of legal advisory services in a wide spectrum of international commercial and corporate activities, with particular focus on financial and maritime services. The firm has been consistently at the forefront of local legislative initiatives and has on several occasions over the years brought about major legislative change in many fields, not least in maritime, ship finance, banking, aviation, trusts and investment services.

*

Richard Wessman is Jur. Dr., Partner, and Head of IP at VINGE. Richard defended his dissertation on trademark law in 2002 at Stockholm University. He has written several articles and books about intellectual property law. He works primarily with agreements and disputes relating to trademarks, company names, design, copyright, marketing and advertising. He has represented clients in a large number of such cases in district courts and courts of appeal, including the Patent and Market Courts, as well as the European Court of Justice. Richard also has extensive experience of teaching at the universities of Stockholm and Uppsala.

Stojan Arnerstål is a lawyer, Counsel and Head of Life Science & Healthcare at VINGE. He has written several articles and books related to trademark law and the licensing of IP, amongst other subjects. Stojan specializes in transactional intellectual property and focuses on legal and strategic advice in matters concerning IP law and contract law. His services primarily focus on IP issues and risk assessments in transactions (M&As), technology transfers, licensing structures and development agreements, including negotiations and drafting. He is in particular experienced in media, technology and life sciences related agreements. Stojan has a background as an academic researcher and was an associate professor (Jur. Dr. and docent) at the Institute of Intellectual Property, Marketing and Competition Law (IMC) at Uppsala University, of which he was also the Director for several years. He regularly teaches at the universities in Uppsala, Stockholm and Lund.

Sofia Bergenstråhle is a Senior Associate at VINGE, specialising in intellectual property law and related matters. Sofia's record of assignments includes the drafting and negotiating of IP agreements and IP work in relation to M&A and public listings, as well as IP litigation matters (e.g. infringement and revocation proceedings). She also has experience from working as a junior judge at the Stockholm District Court and the Patent and Market Court.

VINGE is an independent full-service firm and provides legal advice and leading expertise in all legal and practice areas of business law and is today one of the largest law firms in Sweden. VINGE's IP team is the largest provider of full-service commercial and intellectual property law in Sweden. VINGE's IP team consists of experienced attorneys and lawyers with expertise in all areas of intellectual property law, such as litigation and arbitration, drafting and negotiating intellectual property agreements such as contracts for R&D, licensing, merchandising and franchising and co-existence, management of trademark and design portfolios and due diligence in the context of private and public company acquisitions.

INTRODUCTION

1996 seems like yesterday. It is amazing to see how much has changed since then. April Fool's Day of that year coincided with the first European trade marks being effectively filed in the trade mark world. However, the efforts put into creating the recipient of these filings, namely the European Union Intellectual Property Office (EUIPO) (initially called the Office for Harmonization in the Internal Market or OHIM), were no joke.

Looking back, it is safe to say that these efforts paid off. I cannot resist but to present some numbers: from 46,700 EU trade mark applications in 1996 to 175,000 in 2020. According to the latest statistics, previous records are likely to be broken as the EUIPO received over 101,000 trade mark applications during the first six months of 2021.

EU trade mark law – and by extension, the trade mark law of the EU Member States – has evolved substantially during this period. After numerous directives and regulations harmonizing the substantive law of the Member States and creating the European trade mark, Directive 2004/48/EC of 29 April 2004 on the enforcement of intellectual property rights marked an important step in the European Union's aim to streamline the means of enforcing these rights across the EU.

But the most significant evolution has undoubtedly been the EU Trade Mark Legislative Reform Package, comprising Directive 2015/2436 of 16 December 2015 to approximate the laws of the Member States relating to trade marks (EUTMD) and Regulation 2017/1001 of 14 June 2017 on the European Union trade mark (EUTMR).

Apart from changing the name from 'Community trade mark' to 'EU trade mark', significant changes included the removal of the graphical representation requirement resulting in the acceptance of new types of file to describe the sign for which trade mark protection is sought, such as audio-visual files. This evolution was necessary, as were all the other digitalisation efforts carried out by the EUIPO. However, discussions on whether a particular sign can be protected as a trade mark will not disappear, quite the contrary. The increase of accepted file formats has certainly added complexity to the assessment of the protectable character of a sign as a trade mark.

Another important addition to the legal framework is the incorporation of the CJEU's findings in the *IP Translator* case[1]: the goods and services for which protection is sought must be identified by the applicant with sufficient clarity and precision. The use of general terms to describe the goods and/or services covered by a trade mark application, such as the general indications of the class headings of the Nice Classification, will only cover the literal meaning of the term or indication. All trade mark professionals know the importance of the description of goods and services covered by marks and its impact in trade mark disputes. Increasing clarity in that regard can only be encouraged.

Regarding the EUTMD specifically, it also limited the EU Member States' freedom with regard to their national trade mark law. Various optional provisions became mandatory, such as ensuring that bad faith is taken up as an absolute ground for invalidity. Since 2019, EU Member States must also provide for efficient opposition, revocation and invalidity procedures.

It is interesting to notice that the success of the EU trade mark resulted in a shift from a 'bottom-up' harmonization of national trade mark systems to a 'top-down' approach based on the EU trade mark system. With the EUTMD, EU Member States are now forced to include provisions in their national law which were initially developed for the EU trade mark system.

Apart from the legal framework, another notable evolution relates to the EU case law on trade marks, and more specifically the CJEU case law. Such case law has decreased drastically since 1 May 2019, due to new rules on whether or not to allow appeals to proceed in cases which have already been considered twice. In cases which were already subject to a decision of the EUIPO Board of Appeal and the EU General Court, any appeal must now be accompanied by a request that the appeal be allowed to proceed, not exceeding seven pages, in which the appellant sets out, clearly, the issue raised by the appeal that is significant with respect to the unity, consistency or development of EU law. As a consequence, far fewer appeals have been allowed by the CJEU. As much as we love guidance from Europe's Supreme Court, it is understandable to have filters in place to avoid appeals without sufficient grounds. In any event, the abundant case law of the EU General Court should continue to provide sufficient guidance in the future.

---

1 Judgment of the CJEU of 19 June 2012, *IP Translator*, C-307/10, EU:C:2012:361.

Of course, one of the reasons for the success and increasing numbers of EU trade mark applications has been the expansion of the European Union over the past quarter of a century. 13 Member States joined since the first European trade marks, and sadly one left. This is why a book celebrating the 25th anniversary of the EU trade mark had to include the views of trade mark experts from all over Europe.

This book starts with two contributions about the EUIPO's convergence efforts with the national trade mark offices and the impact of EU case law on national trade mark practice, respectively. It ends with an analysis of the impact of Brexit on EU trade marks.

In between these contributions, the evolution of the EU trade mark system is addressed through a wide variety of subjects of substantive law: trade mark functions, the distinctive character of a trade mark, signs which consist exclusively of the shape of the goods as an absolute ground for refusal of a trade mark, genuine use of a trade mark and its impact on the scope of protection, unregistered trade mark rights, bad faith registration, and misleading use of a trade mark.

Two more contributions cover procedural issues: appropriate jurisdiction of trade mark related disputes, and provisional and protective measures against EU trade mark infringement.

I believe that the wide variety of topics provides for a worthy celebration of the 25th birthday of the EU mark.

I thank all the authors for their endeavours. I also particularly express my appreciation to Diégo Noesen for his help in the follow-up of the editing and production of this book.

Flip PETILLION

I. COOPERATION MILESTONES OF THE "EUROPEAN UNION INTELLECTUAL PROPERTY NETWORK" (EUIPN) ON THE CELEBRATION OF 25 YEARS OF THE EUIPO

Andreea Bende and Ana-Maria Baciu

25 years ago, April 1996 marked a milestone in the history of the intellectual property world, with the filing of the first Community trade mark (nowadays called the EU trade mark). This was made possible through the creation of the European Union Intellectual Property Office (EUIPO), functioning at the time as the Office for Harmonization in the Internal Market (OHIM), one of the six agencies established under the Treaty of the European Union.

The EUIPO was established in 1993 as a decentralized EU agency, having as its main role administering the EU trade mark and Community Design rights throughout the EU (which comprised at the time only 15 Member States).

After the successful launch of the EU trade mark system, the EUIPO also finalized in April 2003 the launch of the Community Design system, registering the first Community design, and thus marking the first important step in the creation of unitary design rights throughout the Member States.

Given the unexpected success and popularity of the EU trade mark system, which exceeded everyone's expectations, the EUIPO subsequently faced many other challenges that required a considerable amount of work and preparation, especially considering the Office's commitment to maintain a certain standard of quality, a fast and effective timeframe for processing applications and administrative procedures (such as oppositions and appeals), and the requirement to make available all of its services and features in all the languages of the EU.

It is worthwhile mentioning, as key moments in the evolution of the EUIPO, the accession in 2004 of 10 new Member States to the EU, followed in 2007 by the accession of Romania and Bulgaria, the creation of the European Observatory, which was fully entrusted to the EUIPO in June 2012, the Trade Mark Reform Package published in 2015, which entered into force in March 2016. Last but not least, we note the activities of **the Cooperation Fund**, which practically jumpstarted the Office's continuous cooperation and collaboration with national and regional intellectual property offices and user associations, resulting in the creation of the European Union Intellectual Property Network (EUIPN).

The creation of the convergence of practices throughout the EU trade mark and design networks was from the beginning a role embraced by the Office, being clearly identified as an on-going objective in the Office's **2011 – 2015 Strategic Plan**[2], which already anticipated that the concrete results expected to be delivered by the various projects tackled by the Cooperation Fund would be already visible prior to the end of 2015.

This role as a convergence facilitator later became one of the EUIPO's statutory tasks, with the adoption of Regulation (EU) 2017/1001, which discusses, under para. (34) of its preamble the necessity to "*[...] establish an appropriate framework for cooperation between the Office and the industrial property offices of the Member States, including the Benelux Office for Intellectual Property, defining key areas of cooperation and enabling the Office to coordinate relevant common projects of interest to the Union and the Member States and to finance, up to a maximum amount, those projects*". The Regulation further states that said "*cooperation activities should be beneficial for undertakings using trade mark systems in Europe. For users of the Union regime laid down in this Regulation, the projects, particularly the databases for search and consultation purposes, should provide additional, inclusive, efficient tools that are free of charge to comply with the specific requirements arising from the unitary character of the EU trade mark.*"

On the celebration of the Office's quarter century from the first EU trade mark applications, we intend to briefly bring together the Office's accomplishments in the field of cooperation with both national intellectual property offices, as well as user associations, and to provide our considerations on the practical outcomes and the impact that such programs had on the users of the trade marks system.

Having said the above, one of the first practical results offered to key users by the Cooperation Fund materialized in the launch of **TM View**[3], a free of

---

2 Https://euipo.europa.eu/tunnel-web/secure/webdav/guest/document_library/contentPdfs/about_ohim/strategic_plan/strategic_plan_en.pdf

3 Https://www.tmdn.org/tmview/#/tmview

charge Internet tool offering the possibility to search for trade marks in a real-time database with information collected from the offices that signed up to the project, available to users since 2010.

Nowadays, TM View features information with respect to over 55 million trade marks from 70 participating offices. From a user's perspective, the tool offers rapid results, which prove valuable towards preliminary conclusions on the chances of success in registering a particular sign as a trade mark in a certain jurisdiction or when the desire is to identify the likelihood of collision with third party intellectual property rights when accessing a new market.

However, from the Romanian market perspective, the tool is not always fully reliable, as it was found over time to also include information that was not updated in terms of certain trade marks' actual status on the Romanian register.

TM View's sister project is **Design View**[4], available from 2012, also offering free of charge access to data relating to designs filed/registered in various countries that implemented the project. The tool proves to be useful not only to users wishing to research the availability of a certain design, but also to examiners from national and regional offices, when performing the examination of the novelty and individual character of design applications.

Another important tool that needs to be mentioned is **TM Class**[5], rebranded in June 2013 from EuroClass, as a consequence of the tool's development and expansion to service classification needs simultaneously from multiple jurisdictions.

In addition to the various tools implemented and made available through the European Union Intellectual Property Network (EUIPN), the result of the cooperation between intellectual property offices and user associations, under the coordination of the EUIPO, aimed at agreeing upon the convergence of trade mark examination practices and at ensuring that the same standards and principles are adopted and applied throughout all Member States, offering a harmonized landscape for all users of the trade marks system, irrespective of their country of origin or their targeted "destination" for seeking trade mark protection.

Each of the convergence programs targeted important issues and, following their implementation and adoption by national offices, changed considerably the trade

4 Https://www.tmdn.org/tmdsview-web/#/dsview.

5 Https://euipo.europa.eu/ec2/.

mark practices landscape and how the same key aspects relating thereto were actually dealt with in local practice and also in the procedures before the EUIPO.

Focused on trade marks, the first Convergence Project (CP) that was finalized is CP1[6] and relates to the **Harmonization on Trade Marks Classification Practice of Goods and Services**. The necessity to adopt a common communication in this field, agreed and embraced by all national offices throughout the EU, derived from the inconsistencies encountered in practice in terms of classification, differing from one national office to the other, especially in terms of the offices' acceptance of applications seeking protection for class headings, as well as regarding the classification of goods which fall outside the alphabetical lists. As a result of the efforts put together by participants in this convergence project, the taxonomy was implemented in TM Class and a Harmonized Database (HDB)[7] was created, allowing users to search through 85,000 pre-validated terms, organized hierarchically. It is thus easier for applicants to classify more correctly the goods and services for which they wish to register their marks and ultimately to anticipate which issues they might encounter in practice before the different offices where they file the same application.

CP1 has also resulted in a common communication on the implementation of the Court's ruling delivered on 19/06/2012 in Case C-307/10 "IP Translator"[8], which stated, among others, that "*an applicant for a national trade mark who uses all the general indications of a particular class heading of the Nice Classification to identify the goods or services for which the protection of the trade mark is sought must specify whether its application for registration is intended to cover all the goods or services included in the alphabetical list of that class or only some of those goods or services. If the application concerns only some of those goods or services, the applicant is required to specify which of the goods or services in that class are intended to be covered.*"

This ruling generated debates amongst users of the trade marks system and resulted in a division of the trade mark applications designating the class headings of the Nice Classification, which were separated in practice into groups of applications filed before or after the "IP Translator".

From a practical perspective, the common communication revealed how each office would interpret applications designating class headings. For example, the Romanian authority regarded applications seeking protection for an entire class heading to include both the goods or services falling within the literal

6 Https://www.tmdn.org/#/practices/1819703.
7 Https://euipo.europa.eu/ohimportal/en/harmonised-database.
8 Https://curia.europa.eu/juris/document/document.jsf?docid=124102&doclang=EN.

interpretation of the class heading, and the goods or services covered by the alphabetical list of that particular class. This practice shifted, however, in July 2020, with the latest amendment of the Romanian Law on Trade marks no. 84/1998, republished, the current interpretation being that class heading applications only cover the goods that fall within their literal meaning.

Moving forward in our overview of Convergence Projects, and without aiming to minimise the importance of each project and its practical results, we have opted to further present the project relating to the **Scope of Protection of Black and White Marks – CP4**[9] – which dealt with a question that many trade mark professionals have received over the years from clients. This relates to whether or not it is sufficient to protect a trade mark in a black & white depiction if it would be also or mainly used in a colour combination, and, respectively, the implications that such a situation would pose to the trade mark's genuine use, to priority claims and to conflicts relying upon the relative grounds provided by law.

At the end of this project, the national offices and user associations created a set of guidelines which should enable users of the trade mark system and, in particular, examiners working for national offices and at the EUIPO, to better assess the question of identity between black and white and colour trade marks. More precisely, the conclusions drawn by the project considered that a mark in a colour variant would be regarded identical to its black and white version only if the differences between both signs are insignificant and only if such differences would be noticed by the average consumer upon their side-by-side examination. As regards the assessment of genuine use, the guidelines conclude that it can be established when use of a black and white trade mark occurred in a colour variant, as long as certain criteria are met: i) the word/figurative elements coincide and are the main distinctive elements; ii) the contrast of shades is respected; iii) the combination of colours does not have a distinctive character in itself; and/or, iv) colour is not one of the main contributors to the overall distinctiveness of the mark.

From the publication of the common practice in 2015, the guidelines and principles comprised therein have been echoed in the relevant case-law of national offices. Once again, offering an example from the Romanian jurisdiction, it may be worthwhile noting that the Romanian Supreme Court failed to grant the required importance to the guidelines set forth by this common communication as when asked to draw on the guidelines thereof, the court stated in its ruling no. 540/2015, issued in the case file no. 5737/3/2012,

---

9 Https://www.tmdn.org/#/practices/1819712.

that "*the appellant's requests [...], in the sense that this court should also refer to the Common Communication on the practice regarding the extension of use of black and white trade marks of 15 April 2014, as well as on the Common Communication on the practice of regarding the relative grounds for refusal – the risk of confusion and the impact of non-distinctive / weak elements therefor, of 2 October 2014, also published by the Romanian State Office for Inventions and Trade mark (SOIT), cannot be received.*

Thus, these communications (subsequent to the ruling date of the appealed decision) are addressed to the national administrative authority with attributions in the field of trade mark registration (SOIT), and do not constitute reasons of public order to be analysed directly in the appeal stage; in addition, the obligation for national courts to harmonize the provisions of European Directives concerns the case law of the EU courts – the Court of First Instance of the European Union and the EU Court of Justice, which censors the practice of the community administrative body (EUIPO) and possibly validates such through the adopted decisions. [...]".[10] Thus, while the Romanian national intellectual property office has adopted said common practice, at least in principle, genuine use is more extensively reviewed at court level in our jurisdiction, and we are yet to see the principles thereof being recognized in the relevant case law of the Romanian courts.

Another important Convergence Project that is linked with CP4 is **CP8**[11], which focuses on the **Use of a Trade Mark in a Form Differing from the one Registered.**

Work on the project started in October 2017 and its main objective was to identify general principles and align the practices of national offices with respect to the genuine use assessment, in particular in cases when use occurred in a form different than the one protected. Various scenarios were identified during the project as common occurrences when dealing in practice with such assessments, such as i) addition of elements to the sign protected; ii) omission of elements from the sign protected; iii) alteration/modification of elements of the sign protected; and iv) a combination of the above.

The common communication that resulted from this conversion project was published in October 2020 and offers important practical examples of assessment structured on the changes listed above – Additions, Omissions, Modifications

---

10 For further details please visit – https://legeaz.net/spete-civil-iccj-2015/decizia-540-2015-ieq (the text is available only in Romanian).

11 Https://www.tmdn.org/#/practices/1819727.

of Characteristics (e.g., typeface, size, colours, position) and a Combination of changes.[12]

While there is, once again, rather scarce recent case-law available in the Romanian jurisdiction referencing the common communication, the principles identified therein can also be found in older jurisprudence, for example, ruling no. 680/2010 issued by the Romanian Supreme Court in February 2010, which states, amongst others: "*The actual use must target the trade mark as it was registered. Even if this principle is not expressly mentioned in the law, it is deduced from art. 46 para. (1) lit. b), which provides that: "It is assimilated to the actual use of the mark (...) the use of the mark in a form that differs from that registered by certain elements that do not alter its distinctive character." It cannot be inferred from this that any similarity between the registered trade mark and that used prevents the cancellation of the trade mark rights, as the appellate court notes. In order to prevent cancellation, the proprietor shall be required to prove the use of the mark exactly as it was registered or in a form different from that in which it was registered by certain elements which do not alter its distinctive character.* "

We will finish our foray into the Conversion Projects launched and finalized by the EUIPO as part of the Office's role in facilitating the harmonization of trade practices by presenting CP11, a project relating to **New Types of Marks and their examination of Formal Requirements and Grounds for Refusal.**[13]

The project's necessity was triggered by the fact that signs which may constitute trade marks were given a new definition in Directive (EU) 2015/2436 of 16 December 2015 on the approximation of the laws of the Member States relating to trade marks, under Art. 3 of the Directive, according to which the requirement that the signs be represented graphically on the register was replaced by the requirement for signs to be represented in the register in a way that allows the competent authorities and the public to clearly and precisely determine the scope of protection. The new definition was subsequently also adopted in the EU Regulation 2017/1001, and opened the gateway for applicants to seek protection of a wider range of signs as trade marks, such as sound marks, marks composed of a single colour or a combination of colours, marks protecting a certain position (on the product or packaging) ("position marks"), marks protecting a certain pattern, marks that highlight the change of position of certain elements ("motion marks"), multimedia marks (combining sounds

---

12 Https://euipo.europa.eu/tunnel-web/secure/webdav/guest/document_library/contentPdfs/about_euipo/who_we_are/common_communication/common_communication_cp8_en.pdf.

13 Https://www.tmdn.org/#/practices/1819734.

and images), holographic marks and other unconventional marks (where we include olfactory, gustatory, tactile marks and layout marks).

Although the project was launched only recently it has already resulted in a Common Communication that was issued in April 2021 and is currently available in the EUIPN portal[14] together with its annexes, offering structured information regarding the definitions and means of representation for different types of mark and the acceptable electronic file formats at the level of national offices, along with the principles of the common practice adopted at the project's completion. The latter are structured based on the examination of formal requirements, the examination of the absolute grounds for refusal and/ or invalidity and, respectively, the examination of relative grounds for refusal and / or invalidity.

The document offers valuable principles especially in connection to borderline cases, in which the examiner has to review from an absolute grounds perspective applications that combined elements pertaining to more than one new type of trade mark, or more delicate aspects such as priority filings in jurisdictions which do not accept the same file formats as supporting documents.

Although the changes brought about by the introduction of new types of trade mark are not yet highly visible in the practice of the Romanian authority, we expect such to trigger important new case-law, especially as regards the assessment of relative grounds conflicts which involve different categories of marks.

Also, while the documents available on the EUIPN network offer clarifications in connection to the technical challenges brought about by the adoption of the possibility to request the registration of these new types of trade mark, users should expect challenges deriving from the different requirements currently imposed by the national offices. For example, until recently, the Romanian office allowed figurative marks to be supported only by.gif file formats. This changed once the office fully migrated to the e-filing applications also accepting different types of marks, which can be currently filed based on various support file formats, depending on the trade mark type.

Looking at the results of past cooperation projects launched and coordinated by the EUIPO, of which we have presented only a few in this article, it gives

---

14 Https://euipo.europa.eu/tunnel-web/secure/webdav/guest/document_library/contentPdfs/EUIPN/CP11/common_communication_cp11_en.pdf.

us confidence that there are even more benefits to come in the future, with the Office continuing its harmonization efforts.

Where some are more acclaimed than others and all are debated thoroughly amongst key users and professionals in the field, we are confident that the common practices aligned throughout the national offices bring more benefits to the network.

The EUIPO appears to be committed to continue its role in the field of cooperation and to expand even more the activities performed under the EUIPN, an aspect which clearly derives from its 2025 Strategic Plan.[15] The plan includes no less than 15 new working groups focused on newly approved European Cooperation Projects (ECPs), amongst which is **ECP2** – aimed at bringing improvements to TM View and Design View, to back office and front office and to facilitate a more extensive use of collaborative work tools, **ECP3** – tasked to be a support group for the IT infrastructure of intellectual property offices through cloud computing, Decision Desktop and Integrated Multiple Assessment Solution, **ECP4** – having within its remit the Convergence Analysis 2.0 and the maintenance of existing common practices, **ECP5** – offering support to the Project and Quality Management Development and Emerging Technologies Incubator and **ECP7** – aiming to create an intellectual property legislative and practice repository.

Looking both at the past as well as towards the future, it is more than obvious that the work, efforts and resources allocated by the EUIPO to the optimization, efficiency and overall progress of the EU trade marks system, has shaped and will continue to shape the overall intellectual property landscape of the European Union and internationally, the Office today having made a giant leap from the first EU trade mark application received 25 years ago.

15 Https://euipo.europa.eu/tunnel-web/secure/webdav/guest/document_library/contentPdfs/about_euipo/strategic_plan/SP2025_en.pdf

II. HOW HAS EUIPO PRACTICE AFFECTED NATIONAL ADMINISTRATIVE TRADE MARK PRACTICE IN THE EU MEMBER STATES?

Claus Barrett CHRISTIANSEN and Maria Rose KRISTENSEN

The Community Trade Mark Regulation (the 'Regulation')[16] was adopted by the Council of the European Union in December 1993 and came into force in March 1994. The Regulation created the European Trade Mark (EUTM, formerly known as the 'Community Trade Mark' or CTM) and established the EUIPO (formerly known as the OHIM).

More than two years went by after the commencement of the Regulation before the first European Trade Mark application was filed on 1 April 1996, and more than 25 years have now gone by since the filing of the first EUTM application.

With the EUTM system, it became possible to file *one* trade mark application and obtain protection throughout the entire EU, instead of filing separate trade mark applications in each of the EU Member States. The new system quickly became a huge success, and by the end of 1996[17] 46,700 EUTM applications had been filed.

With the huge success – and as time went by – came various decisions relating to EUTMs from the EUIPO, the Boards of Appeal (BoA), the General Court (GC) and the European Court of Justice (CJEU) that could not be ignored by the national trade mark offices[18], as the national trade mark offices were obligated to protect the EUTMs at national level on a par with national trade mark registrations and to follow decisions from the GC and the CJEU according to the

16 COUNCIL REGULATION (EC) No 40/94 of 20 December 1993.

17 Https://euipo.europa.eu/ohimportal/en/our-history.

18 The reference to national trade mark offices in this article does also include the Benelux Office for Intellectual Property ('BOIP').

EU Treaty. Additionally, the Member States' national trade mark acts originated from the Trade Mark Directive of 1988[19], which meant that the national trade mark offices were bound by the CJEU's preliminary rulings on the interpretation of the Trade Mark Directive.

1. THE FIRST DECADE

A. BABY-DRY VS. DOUBLEMINT

During the first years of the EUTM system, it became clear that it was no easy task for the national trade mark offices to blindly follow the EUIPO's practice, and nor did most national trade mark offices wish to do so.

A perfect example of this is the BABY-DRY case.[20] During the early 1990s Procter & Gamble applied for registration of the trade mark BABY-DRY (word) for '*disposable diapers made out of paper or cellulose and diapers made out of textile*' in various EU Member States, and obtained registrations in Member States such as France and Denmark. With the new EUTM system, Procter & Gamble wanted to try their luck, and in April 1996 they applied for EUTM registration of the trade mark BABY-DRY (word). However, the EUIPO refused the trade mark application in January 1998, and the BoA later dismissed the appeal brought by Procter & Gamble, as the BoA found that the trade mark BABY-DRIVE consisted exclusively of words that may serve, in trade, to designate the intended purpose of the goods, and also the BoA found BABY-DRY devoid of distinctive character, and the trade mark was therefore not eligible for registration under Article 7(1)(b) and (c) of the Regulation. The GC later upheld the BoA's decision, and Procter & Gamble appealed to the CJEU.

National trade mark offices in many of the EU Member States, including France and Denmark, were anxiously awaiting the decision of the CJEU, as the practices of the EUIPO, the BoA and the GC went against their national practices for assessing descriptiveness. In September 2001 the ruling of the CJEU was delivered, and some national offices could breathe a sigh of relief: the CJEU annulled the decision of the GC, concluding that the trade mark BABY-DRY was capable of constituting a EUTM, *inter alia* by stating that BABY-DRY constituted a *lexical invention*, a new characteristic of a trade mark never heard of before. For other national offices, the CJEU decision broke with strong national practices for assessing distinctiveness and descriptiveness.

19 First Council Directive 89/104/EEC of 21 December 1988.

20 Judgement of the CJEU of 20 September 2001 in case C-383/99 between Procter & Gamble and EUIPO.

However, things soon got blurred, as a CJEU decision concerning the same topic saw the light of day in October 2003 in the DOUBLEMINT case.[21] In this case, Wrigley applied for registration of DOUBLEMINT (word) as a EUTM for, e.g., *'chewing gum'* in March 1996. Like Procter & Gamble in the BABY-DRY case, Wrigley had obtained national trade mark registrations for the trade mark DOUBLEMINT (word) in various Member States in the EU prior to the filing of the EUTM application. Despite this – and in line with its decision in the BABY-DRY case – the EUIPO rejected the registration, as DOUBLEMINT in their opinion was not eligible for registration under Article 7(1)(b) and (c) of the Regulation. The EUIPO's decision was upheld by the BoA, but Wrigley did not give up and decided to bring an action for annulment against the BoA's decision before the GC in September 1999. The GC concluded that the word DOUBLEMINT, when applied to the goods referred to in the application, had an ambiguous and suggestive meaning that was open to various interpretations, and it did not enable the public concerned to detect the description of a characteristic of the goods in question immediately and without further reflection. Since it was not exclusively descriptive, the term could not, according to the GC, be refused registration, and accordingly the GC annulled the BoA's decision. No mention was made of *lexical invention* but it was still in line with the CJEU's decision in BABY-DRY.

The decision of the GC was appealed to the CJEU by the EUIPO, but after the CJEU's decision in the BABY-DRY case in September 2001 most commentators and national offices expected that the CJEU would uphold the decision of the GC. The CJEU decision was handed down in October 2003, and to the surprise of many the CJEU annulled the GC's decision and argued that DOUBLEMINT consisted exclusively of words that may serve, in trade, to designate the intended purpose of the goods, that it was also devoid of distinctive character, and that it was therefore not eligible for registration.

The question now was what the different outcomes of the BABY-DRY case and the DOUBLEMINT case would mean to the future practices of the EU Member States and the EUIPO?

The EUIPO and some national offices, including the offices of the United Kingdom and Germany, took the view that the DOUBLEMINT case overruled the CJEU's precedence in the BABY-DRY decision. The view of the EUIPO was not a surprise, as according to the EUIPO the CJEU had just confirmed the EUIPO's original assessment in the DOUBLEMINT case. Neither was the view of the trade mark offices of the United Kingdom and Germany a surprise, as the

21 Judgement of the CJEU of 23 October 2003 in case C-191/01 between Wm. Wrigley Jr. and EUIPO.

decision in the DOUBLEMINT case in their opinion aligned the EUTM system more closely with the practices of their national offices. The governments of both the UK and Germany had intervened in support of the EUIPO before the CJEU in the DOUBLEMINT case. The German national office had previously denied registration of trade marks such as DOUBLE COLOR and DOUBLE ACTION with reference to their exclusively descriptive character, and the DOUBLEMINT decision fit in well with this practice.

Other trade mark offices – such as the Danish trade mark office – took the view that both decisions were to live side by side as a joint contribution to the future practices of the EUIPO and the national offices in the EU. Thus, the Danish trade mark office still found support for their original national decision of registering BABY-DRY as a national trade mark.

Although Germany and the United Kingdom chose to side with the EUIPO in the BABY-DRY/DOUBLEMINT cases, the trade mark offices of Germany and the United Kingdom did not blindly follow the practice of the EUIPO during the first decade of the EUIPO. As the body of decisions from the EUIPO and the BoA grew, it became more and more clear that the gap between the practices of the national offices and the EUIPO was widening.

B. NEW EU MEMBER STATES IN 2004

In May 2004, ten countries joined the EU, and the EU Member States went from 15 to 25. The countries joining were Cyprus, Estonia, Latvia, Lithuania, Malta, Poland, Slovakia, Slovenia, the Czech Republic and Hungary.

The main legal consequence of the expansion of the EU for holders of EUTMs filed before the date of the enlargement was that their protection as a main rule was automatically extended to the territories of the new Member States. This meant that more than 300,000 EUTMs were extended and were now also enforceable in the new Member States.[22]

The majority of the new EU Member States belonged to Eastern and Central Europe. Most of the new Member States did not have well-developed trade mark systems or practices, and as such their approach was to more or less copy the practice and guidelines of the EUIPO, with the result that the differences between the practices of these national trade mark offices and the practice of the EUIPO was almost non-existent.

22 Communication No 05/03 of the President of the Office of 16 October 2003.

Hence, with the expansion of the EU, the EUIPO gained further support for its administrative practices, which were copied to a wide extent by most of the new national offices. But that did not mean that the EUIPO could get away with anything...

2. IP TRANSLATOR

There was still a substantial gap between the practices of many of the national offices, especially the older ones, and the practice of the EUIPO, and one battlefield was the 'class headings cover all' approach versus the 'what you see is what you get' approach when it came to the administrative interpretation of the Nice Classification's class headings.

In June 2003, the president of the EUIPO issued a communication[23] stating that the use of class headings in the specification of a EUTM application or registration meant that all goods and/or services that fall within that class are covered by the EUTM application or registration – the 'class headings cover all' approach.

The approach of the EUIPO went directly against the practices of several strong national trade mark offices[24], and in an effort to address the differing positions and stand up to the EUIPO, the British Chartered Institute of Patent Attorneys (CIPA) filed a trade mark application for IP TRANSLATOR (word) for the services covering '*education; providing of training; entertainment; sporting and cultural activities*' (the class heading for class 41) with the national trade mark office of the United Kingdom. The CIPA's co-conspirator, the UK national office, set aside its usual 'what you see is what you get' approach in the service of a higher cause and refused the trade mark application, arguing that it was descriptive of '*translation services*', which fell under class 41. The CIPA appealed the decision to the Person Appointed by the Lord Chancellor under Section 76 of the UK Trademarks Act ('Appointed Person'), contending that its application for IP TRANSLATOR had been wrongly denied, as the application did not specify, and therefore did not cover, '*translation services*' in class 41.

The Appointed Person drafted a reference for a preliminary ruling from the CJEU[25], asking the CJEU the following three questions:

---

23 Communication No 4/03 of the President of the Office of 16 June 2003.

24 See Table 1 in Common Communication on the Implementation of 'IP Translator' v1. 2, 20 February 2014.

25 C-307/10.

1. Is it necessary for the various goods or services covered by a trade mark application to be identified with any, and if so what particular, degree of clarity and precision?
2. Is it permissible to use the general words of the class headings of the Nice Classification for the purpose of identifying the various goods or services covered by a trade mark application?
3. Is it necessary or permissible for such use of the general words of the Class Headings of the Nice Classification to be interpreted in accordance with Communication No 4/03?

Various submissions were made to the CJEU during the IP TRANSLATOR case by various parties, thus confirming the importance of the case. Besides submissions from the CIPA and the EUIPO, there were submissions from the European Commission and eleven Member States.

In the EUIPO's submission, the EUIPO not only argued in favour of their practice as communicated in Communication 4/03, it also argued that the reference for a preliminary ruling should be declared inadmissible on the grounds that it was artificial. Such arguments showed a desire on the part of the EUIPO to avoid a decision on the issue at all costs, as they were willing to go far to keep their practice in force. The CJEU did, however, allow the reference, and in June 2012 the CJEU answered the three questions:

1. The Trade Mark Directive of 2008[26] must be interpreted as meaning that it requires the goods and services for which the protection of the trade mark is sought to be identified by the applicant with sufficient clarity and precision to enable the competent authorities and economic operators, on that basis alone, to determine the extent of the protection conferred by the trade mark.
2. The Trade Mark Directive of 2008 must be interpreted as meaning that it does not preclude the use of the general indications of the class headings of the Nice Classification to identify the goods and services for which the protection of the trade mark is sought, provided that such identification is sufficiently clear and precise.
3. An applicant for a national trade mark who uses all the general indications of a particular class heading of the Nice Classification to identify the goods or services for which the protection of the trade mark is sought must specify whether its application for registration is intended to cover all the goods or services included in the alphabetical list of that class or only some of those goods or services. If the application concerns only some of those goods or

[26] Directive 2008/95/EC of the European Parliament and of the Council of 22 October 2008.

services, the applicant is required to specify which of the goods or services in that class are intended to be covered.

The answers made it very clear that the previous practice of the EUIPO as communicated in Communication 4/03 was in violation of the Trade Mark Regulation.

The EUIPO was forced to change its practice, and less than 24 hours after the CJEU's ruling, the EUIPO announced that its communication of June 2003 had been repealed and replaced by a new communication.[27] In line with the CJEU's decision, the communication confirmed, however, that in future the EUIPO would continue to accept the use of the general indications of the class headings on a case-by-case basis. In this respect, the EUIPO announced that it would update its filing system in order for the users to declare whether or not they claimed protection for all goods and/or services in the alphabetical list of the Nice Classification when using the general indications of the class headings. As for existing registrations, changing practices retroactively seemed unimaginable.

One of the masterminds of the IP TRANSLATOR case, the trade mark office of the United Kingdom, still chose to apply a practice different from the amended communication issued by the EUIPO. In its Practice Amendment Notice[28] the UK trade mark office declared that if an applicant wished to obtain protection of all goods or services in the alphabetical list of one class, it was not enough to declare this when using the general indications of the class headings. Instead, the applicant was obliged explicitly to name the goods and services of the alphabetical list that the application was intended to cover.

3. A TIME FOR COOPERATION

The diverging positions of the first decade as demonstrated by the examples above proved that cooperation between the EUIPO and the national trade mark offices was essential. Venues for such cooperation were established and developed on an ongoing basis, for instance the Liaison Meetings.

The Liaison Meetings take place four times a year, and two of the four meetings revolve around trade mark issues. The meetings are held between the EUIPO and the national trade mark offices to discuss issues of common interest and to

27 Communication No 2/12 of the President of the Office of 20 June 2012.
28 Practice Amendment Notice 01/12 of July 2012 (came into force on 30 July 2012).

exchange best practices. Since 2011, the Liaison Meetings have had an important role in the development of the so-called Convergence Programmes.

2011 was also the year when the European Union Intellectual Property Network (EUIPN) (formerly known as the European Trade Mark and Design Network) was established, bringing together the EUIPO, the national trade mark offices of the EU and international partners, with an aim to create tools and online services as well as to harmonise practices.

A. DEVELOPMENT OF THE CONVERGENCE PROGRAMMES

The harmonisation of practices has been developed primarily through the Convergence Programmes that quickly became the heart of the EUIPN.

The Convergence Programmes are a series of programmes developed by the EUIPO, the national trade mark offices of the EU and international partners in the network in order to try to find common ground in areas where diverging practices exist. The aim is to limit – if not eliminate – situations where similar trade mark and design applications are treated differently[29] by the EUIPO and the national offices of the Member States. IP Translator conflicts should be avoided through dialogue and common practices.

This year the EUIPN has celebrated its 10-year anniversary, and at the same time the EUIPN can celebrate the publication of no less than 12 Convergence Programmes, with more in the pipeline:

- CP1 – Harmonisation of Trade Mark Classification Practice of Goods and Services
- CP2 – Convergence of Class Headings
- CP3 – Absolute Grounds for Refusal of Figurative Trade Marks with Purely Descriptive Words or Expressions
- CP4 – Scope of Protection of Trade Marks Exclusively in Black, White and/or Shades of Grey
- CP5 – Relative Grounds and Likelihood of Confusion (the impact of non-distinctive/weak components)
- CP6 – Convergence on Graphic Representations of Designs
- CP7 – Harmonization of the Product Indications

[29] Https://euipo.europa.eu/ohimportal/en/strategic-drivers/ipnetwork/european-cooperation.

CP8 – Use of a trade mark in a form differing from the one registered
CP9 – Distinctiveness of shape marks containing other elements when the shape itself is not distinctive
CP10 – Criteria for assessing the disclosure of designs on the Internet
CP11 – New types of marks: examination of formal requirements and grounds for refusal
CP12 – Evidence in trade mark appeal proceedings

It is an accepted fact that the development of the Convergence Programmes is a consequence of the ongoing pressure placed on the EUIPO from national trade mark offices in areas of diverging practices that came to a head in the IP TRANSLATOR case. This is also evident from the first two Convergence Programmes, which dealt with the classification of goods and services and class headings.

The EUIPN and the Convergence Programmes are the national trade mark offices' opportunity to influence the EUIPO when it comes to diverging practices. Not all trade mark offices take advantage of this opportunity, and the level of engagement of the national offices varies.

When the EUIPN was first established, it was optional whether or not the national trade mark offices would participate in the development of the Convergence Programmes. With the EU Trade Mark Regulation of 2017[30], participation became obligatory.[31] However, the obligation to participate does not guarantee a high level of engagement (or influence) from each of the national offices within the EU, and where it is the case that national offices have simply decided to blindly follow EUIPO practice, it is not obvious why they should spend resources on the development of convergence programmes.

The national offices that wish to influence the development of the Convergence Programmes need to become members of a working group, as each Convergence Project is supported by a working group comprised of representatives from the EUIPO and national trade mark offices in the EU, observers from national trade mark offices outside the EU, representatives from user associations and in some cases representatives from international organisations such as the WIPO. The working group of each project develops a set of common guidelines that reflect a common practice of an area of law. The common guidelines are then presented at a Liaison Meeting, after which they are approved by the Management Board

[30] REGULATION (EU) 2017/1001 OF THE EUROPEAN PARLIAMENT AND OF THE COUNCIL of 14 June 2017 (EUTMR).

[31] See EUTMR Article 152.

of the EUIPO. Once the common guidelines are approved, they are published as common communications on the websites of the EUIPO and the national trade mark offices.

Even if a national office is represented in a working group, its influence is not guaranteed per se. Despite what could be expected, the voting power of the national offices does not reflect either their population or the EUTMs filed from that particular Member State. Instead, influence seems to depend on the involvement of the respective Member State, reflecting its knowledge and its involvement in the discussions of the working groups. Even the national offices of small countries, such as Denmark, seem to be able to affect the content of the common communications at the same level as large national offices of countries such as Spain or Italy.

B. THE CONVERGENCE PROGRAMMES IN PRACTICE

The importance of the Convergence Programmes is undisputed when it comes to the practices of the EUIPO, which has decided to incorporate the common practices of the Convergence Programmes in its official guidelines.

On the other hand, some of the national trade mark offices are struggling with the implementation of the Convergence Programmes, as the Programmes are not a source of law.

For some trade mark offices it has been customary that each of their caseworkers have their 'own' practice, which has made it very difficult to implement the Convergence Programmes in such regimes.

Other trade mark offices have successfully implemented the Convergence Programmes in their practice but do not see their boards of appeal adopting the Convergence Programmes. One of these trade mark offices is the Danish Patent and Trademark Office (DKPTO), which has encountered the reluctance of the Danish Board of Appeal for Patents and Trademarks ('Danish Board of Appeal') in, for instance, the national cases relating to the trade marks FRILAND (figurative) and FOOD CLUB (figurative).

i) FRILAND and FOOD CLUB

In October 2015, the DKPTO issued a communication[32] confirming that – as of January 2016 – the practice of the DKPTO would be amended in accordance with CP3 – Absolute Grounds for Refusal of Figurative Trade Marks with Purely Descriptive Words or Expressions.

In January 2016, the Danish company Friland A/S applied for registration of the below trade mark[33] for goods and services in classes 29, 30, 42 and 43, a combination of the word element FRILAND and a figure depicting something that could be perceived as an open landscape under a bright sky:

In August 2016, the DKPTO – in accordance with CP3 – refused to register the trade mark in classes 29 and 30 due to lack of distinctiveness. In this respect, the DKPTO found that the word element 'FRILAND' (meaning an area in the open, often used as farmland) was descriptive of the goods in question, and that the figurative element of the trade mark was devoid of distinctive character, as it merely consisted of a basic shape.

The Danish Board of Appeal reversed the decision of the DKPTO, arguing that an overall assessment of the elements of the trade mark lead to a conclusion of distinctiveness. In its decision the Danish Board of Appeal even mentioned the DKPTO's communication of October 2015, but nevertheless decided to go against it and CP3.

---

32 Https://vmguidelines.dkpto.dk/media/102655/brugerbrev%20af%202.%20oktober%202015%20om%20figurm%C3%A6rkers%20s%C3%A6rpr%C3%A6g%20med%20f%C3%A6llesmeddelelse%20fra%20varem%C3%A6rkemyndighederne%20i%20eu.pdf.

33 Danish trade mark application no. VA 2016 00175.

Presumably to the annoyance of the DKPTO, the Danish Board of Appeal took the same approach in the FOOD CLUB case.[34] In December 2017, the Danish company Madklubben ApS applied for registration of the below trade mark[35] for goods and services in classes 32, 33 and 43:

The DKPTO refused to register the trade mark for *'services for providing food and drinks'* in class 43, arguing that the trade mark was devoid of any distinctive characters. In this respect, the DKPTO found that the word elements 'FOOD CLUB' was a term often used for *'services for providing food and drinks'*. Additionally, the DKPTO concluded that cutlery is often used to describe the services in question, and that the use of the square was devoid of distinctiveness as it merely consisted of a basic shape.

Dissatisfied with the decision of the DKPTO, Madklubben Aps brought an appeal before the Danish Board of Appeal. The Danish Board of Appeal found that the trade mark was distinctive due to the figurative elements of the trade marks that were drawn by hand. Consequently, the Danish Board of Appeal reversed the decision of the DKPTO, ignoring the DKPTO's communication of October 2015 and CP3.

ii) KINDER

Today, six years after the publication of the DKPTO's communication, it seems that the Danish Board of Appeal is more attentive to the communication and the CP3. This is reflected in the Danish Board of Appeal's decision in the KINDER case.[36]

In May 2020, the Danish company Arla Foods amba applied for registration of the below trade mark[37] for goods in classes 5 and 29:

---

34 Decision of 14 May 2020 in case AN 2019 00011.

35 Danish trade mark application no. VA 2016 00175.

36 Decision of 12 August 2021 in case AN 2021 00012.

37 Danish trade mark application no. VA 2020 00956.

The DKPTO found that the word element of the trade mark was descriptive of the goods in question and that the figurative elements of the trade marks were non-distinctive. Consequently, the DKPTO denied registration of the trade mark.

Arla Foods amba decided to appeal the decision to the Danish Board of Appeal, arguing that their trade mark was indeed distinctive for the goods in question.

Much to the surprise of the DKPTO, the Danish Board of Appeal upheld the decision of the DKPTO, confirming that the trade mark was devoid of any distinctive character. In this respect, the Danish Board of Appeal concluded that the figurative elements of the trade mark were not able to provide distinctiveness to the trade mark, as their playful stylisation simply emphasised the meaning of the word element (meaning children).

The development from the FRILAND decision and onward 6 years later to the KINDER decision shows the difficulties in implementing substantial changes in national offices and appeal boards, where highly skilled and well-meaning specialists struggle to assess new guidance in an area of law that very much depends on the discretion and interpretation of the specialists. The way that CJEU case law zigzagged at the beginning of the 1990s with BABY-DRY and DOUBLEMINT might also still influence the pace at which change is implemented at the national offices, since a wait-and-see approach has previously proven appropriate.

4. FUTURE COOPERATION

Despite the struggle of some national offices, cooperation within the EUIPN and the Convergence Programmes is today considered a success – in fact even an award-winning success, as the programmes were granted the European Public Service Award in 2017.[38]

[38] In 2017, the EUIPN received the European Public Service Award in the European and regional category for its work on contributing to the emergence of a coherent and streamlined pan-European IP landscape.

In its 2025 Strategic Plan, the EUIPN has eight projects that are to be developed before 2025. The aim of all these projects is to support the complete transposition of the Trade Mark Directive and carry on developing and improving the tools and services developed under previous cooperation iterations.[39] The eight projects are:

ECP1: Consolidate the implementation of EUIPN tools
ECP2: Improvement and upgrade of EUIPN tools
ECP3: New tools
ECP4: Convergence of Practices
ECP5: Sustainability of the Network
ECP6: Supporting SMEs
ECP 7: Implementation of the Directive
ECP8: Collaborative Services

When it comes to ECP4 – Convergence of Practices, one could argue that the need for new Convergence Programmes is not as apparent as before, as the body of guiding case law from the GC and the CJEU is now rather voluminous and very detailed, and practice at the EUIPO is solid.

However, it is the firm belief of the authors of this article that the EUTM system will continue to benefit from further development of the Convergence Programmes, as it represents a strong guidance and a token of co-operation between the EU Member States within the area of trade mark law.

[39] Https://euipo.europa.eu/ohimportal/en/strategic-drivers/ipnetwork/european-cooperation.

III. THE DEVELOPMENT OF THE CONCEPT OF TRADE MARK FUNCTIONS

Jan Peter HEIDENREICH

The development of a concept of (different) trade mark functions in recent years is one of the most significant and potentially far-reaching developments in European – and by implication national – trade mark law. Whilst the idea of a trade mark serving several functions – besides its main function as an indication of origin – has been around for quite some time[40], it has never gained much ground in jurisprudence and has never been developed into a coherent system of trade mark functions by the courts.

This article endeavours to trace the development of the concept of trade mark functions in the jurisprudence of the European Courts, to outline the current status of the doctrine and to – briefly – describe its reception by the EUIPO, the national courts and academia.

1. THE TRADITIONAL NOTION OF TRADE MARK FUNCTION(S)

Traditionally, there was only one trade mark function: The indication of origin of the goods and services[41] marked.[42]

40 There have been discussions in Germany (and Italy) at least since the 1960s, cf. Vanzetti, GRUR Ausl. 1965, 128; Beier, GRUR Int. 1968, 8; Sack, GRUR 1972, 402; Heydt, GRUR 1976, 7; GRUR Int. 1976, 342; see also Kur, BeckOK MarkenR, Einleitung Rn. 118 ff.

41 In the following analysis I will use the term 'goods' as shorthand for 'goods and services'. Thus, unless otherwise noted, the term 'goods' also includes 'services'.

42 Cf. the German Federal Supreme Court judgment in a 1960s case of parallel imports, in which the court ruled that the trade mark owner had no legal recourse against a parallel importer on the grounds that the main function of a trade mark was to indicate the origin of the goods marked, not the owner's interest in controlling the distribution of the goods (GRUR 1964, 372 – Maja).

The notion that a trade mark protects its owner only against such uses by third parties that impair the trade mark's ability to indicate the origin of the goods sets trade mark law apart from other intellectual property rights that are protected regardless of any functions they may have or serve. The protection of a patent or a copyright is absolute; its owner can prohibit any use of a patent or a copyrighted work by an unauthorised third party, regardless of whether that use impairs any 'function' of the patent or copyright. By contrast, a trade mark owner can enjoin others from using their trade mark only if and to the extent that that use impairs a function of the trade mark (traditionally the function of indicating origin). This fundamental principle has not changed with the advent of the notion of different trade mark functions, and the Court of Justice of the European Union (CJEU) has merely expanded the functions a trade mark serves and its owner can invoke against third-party use.

2. RECEPTION OF THAT TRADITIONAL NOTION IN THE JURISPRUDENCE OF THE CJEU

Before the birth of the Community trade mark in 1996 the CJEU had scarce opportunities to adjudicate on trade mark matters. However, cases involving (national) trade marks have reached the Court in several instances, in particular in connection with the fundamental principle of the free movement of goods.

One of the first judgments of the CJEU pertaining to (national) trade marks was the *HAG I* decision of 1974.[43] The facts of the case were rather peculiar, pertaining to identical trade marks of companies formerly under common control but separated in World War II due to the sequestration of a Belgian subsidiary of a German instant coffee producer 'HAG AG'. The question that arose in the case before the CJEU was

> whether the Community rules on competition or those relating to the free movement of goods prohibit the holder of a trade mark enjoying legal protection in a Member State from opposing the importation of products that legally bear "the same trade mark" in another Member State, where at the outset the two marks belonged to the same holder. (para. 2 of the judgment)

The CJEU took a rather critical stance towards trade marks and their exclusivity and held that

[43] Judgment of the CJEU of 3 July 1974, *Van Zuylen v. Hag AG*, C-192/73, ECLI:EU:C:1974:72.

> to prohibit the marketing in a Member State of a product legally bearing a trade mark in another Member State, for the sole reason that an identical trade mark having the same origin[44] exists in the first state, is incompatible with the provisions providing for free movement of goods within the Common Market. (para. 15)

Allowing the holder of a trade mark to rely upon the exclusiveness of a trade mark right and to prohibit the marketing in a Member State of goods legally produced in another Member State under an identical mark would, the Court held, legitimise the isolation of national markets and would therefore collide with one of the essential objects of the Treaty, which is to unite national markets in a single market (paras. 12 and 13). While in such a market the indication of origin of a product covered by a trade mark is useful, information to consumers on this point may be ensured by means other than such as would affect the free movement of goods (para. 14).

Thus, while the CJEU's focus is clearly on the free movement of goods, the function of a trade mark to indicate the origin finds its first mention in its jurisprudence.

The first proper discussion of the function(s) of trade marks was made in the Court's 1978 *Hoffmann-LaRoche* decision[45] (one of the first in a seemingly endless stream of decisions on parallel imports of pharmaceuticals). The CJEU held that

> In order to determine the exact scope of this right exclusively conferred on the owner of the trade-mark, regard must be had to the essential function of the trade mark, which is to guarantee the identity of the origin of the marked product to the consumer or ultimate user by enabling him without any possibility of confusion to distinguish that product from products which have another origin. [...] The right attributed to the proprietor of preventing any use of the trade-mark which is likely to impair the guarantee of origin so understood is therefore part of the specific subject-matter of the trade-mark right. (para. 7, emphasis added)

The basic tenet that the 'essential function' of a trade mark is 'to guarantee the identity of the origin of the marked products' has been repeated and confirmed by the CJEU in numerous judgments.[46]

---

44 This reference is to the origin of the trade marks, not the origin of the goods marked with it.

45 Judgment of the CJEU of 23 May 1978, *Hoffmann-La Roche v. Centrafarm*, C-102/77, ECLI:EU:C:1978:108.

46 See for example the judgment of the CJEU of 17 October 1990, *CNL-SUCAL v. HAG*, C-10/89, ECLI:EU:C:1990:359, paragraph 14; judgment of the CJEU of 22 June 1994, *IHT Internationale Heiztechnik v. Ideal-Standard*, C-9/93, ECLI:EU:C:1994:261, paragraphs 37 and 45.

While the CJEU has, from the beginning, stated that the function of guaranteeing the origin of goods is the 'essential' function of a trade mark and thus by implication not necessarily the only function, the Court has never explicitly acknowledged any other trade mark function before the EU trade mark system came into being.

3. THE DEVELOPMENT OF DIFFERENT TRADE MARK FUNCTIONS UNDER THE EU TRADE MARK SYSTEM

With the arrival of the Trade Mark Directive[47] (TMD) and later the Community Trade Mark Regulation[48] (CTMR), the question of the function(s) of trade marks gained new significance. While before it had been relevant only in the context of the free movement of goods and the justification of limits to that freedom, now the function of trade marks became one of the deciding aspects of determining infringement.

The TMD has for the first time explicitly acknowledged the function of trade marks to indicate the origin of products in its 10th Recital[49]:

> Whereas the protection afforded by a Community trade mark, the function of which is in particular to guarantee the trade mark as an indication of origin...

As the Court had done before it, the EU legislator has thus explicitly accepted (only) the function of indicating the origin, without stating any other (possible) functions of trade mark. But, again like the Court before it, the legislator has also acknowledged that there might be other, additional functions a trade mark might have, as is clear from the phrase 'in particular'.

A. THE FUNCTION OF INDICATING ORIGIN

The CJEU has picked up on the explicit mention of the origin function in the Recitals of the TMD in its 2002 *Arsenal Football Club* judgment.[50]

---

[47] Directive 89/104/EEC of 21 December 1988 to approximate the laws of the Member States relating to trade marks.

[48] Council Regulation (EC) No 40/94 of 20 December 1993 on the Community trade mark.

[49] The CTMR contains identical wording in its 7th Recital.

[50] Judgment of the CJEU of 12 November 2002, *Arsenal Football Club plc v. Matthew Reed*, C-206/01, ECLI:EU:C:2002:651.

As the *Arsenal Football Club* case involved an identical mark for identical goods and the 10th Recital of the TMD explicitly stated that in cases of double identity (identical signs and identical goods) a trade mark's protection was 'absolute', the CJEU's assessment could have ended at that point (with a finding of infringement). However, the court went on to discuss trade mark function(s).

The Court begins by repeating the notion outlined in its *Hoffmann-LaRoche* judgment that the 'essential function' of a trade mark is to indicate the origin:

> [...] the essential function of a trade mark is to guarantee the identity of origin of the marked goods or services to the consumer or end user by enabling him, without any possibility of confusion, to distinguish the goods or services from others which have another origin. For the trade mark to be able to fulfil its essential role in the system of undistorted competition which the Treaty seeks to establish and maintain, it must offer a guarantee that all the goods or services bearing it have been manufactured or supplied under the control of a single undertaking which is responsible for their quality [...] (at para. 48).

The Court then goes on to state that any infringement of a trade mark requires that the trade mark's functions are liable to be impaired by the allegedly infringing act:

> [...] the exclusive right under article 5(1)(a) of the Directive was conferred in order to enable the trade mark proprietor to protect his specific interests as proprietor, that is, to ensure that the trade mark can fulfil its functions. <u>The exercise of that right must therefore be reserved to cases in which a third party's use of the sign affects or is liable to affect the functions of the trade mark</u>, in particular its essential function of guaranteeing to consumers the origin of the goods. (para 51, emphasis added)

The protection granted to trade mark proprietors by article 5(1)(a) TMD in an absolute way was thus explicitly limited to cases in which the trade mark function(s) could be adversely affected[51]:

> The proprietor may not prohibit the use of a sign identical to the trade mark for goods identical to those for which the mark is registered if that use cannot affect his own interests as proprietor of the mark, having regard to its functions. (para. 54)

It is noteworthy that, while the Court refers to trade mark 'functions', only the function of indicating the origin is explicitly named and discussed.

---

51 This is quite explicit in AG Jääskinen's opinion in the case of 13 June 2002 (at para. 60): 'The Directive confers on the registered proprietor a monopoly over the sign which he has registered as a trade mark, but that power of exclusive disposition is, as I have pointed out, relative, because it is at the service of a purpose that transcends it.'

B. THE ADVERTISING FUNCTION

It took until 2009 for the CJEU to acknowledge specific trade mark functions beyond the function of indicating origin. In its *L'Oréal/Bellure* decision[52] the Court held that

> the exclusive right under article 5(1)(a) of Directive 89/104 was conferred in order to enable the trade mark proprietor to protect his specific interests as proprietor, that is, to ensure that the trade mark can fulfil its functions and that, therefore, the exercise of that right must be reserved to cases in which a third party's use of the sign affects or is liable to affect the functions of the trade mark [...]. These functions include not only the essential function of the trade mark, which is to guarantee to consumers the origin of the goods or services, but also its other functions, in particular that of guaranteeing the quality of the goods or services in question and those of communication, investment or advertising. (para. 58, emphasis added)

Thus, while maintaining that the function of indicating origin is the 'essential' function of a trade mark, the Court also (for the first time) recognised an advertising function, an investment function, a communication function and a quality function.

The CJEU did not further elaborate on these additional functions or explain their meaning and scope but merely stated that it was for the national court to decide whether any of these functions were impaired by the use in question. The Court did, however, clarify that the additional functions beyond the function of indicating origin were relevant only in the case of an identical mark being used for identical goods and that for the assessment of the likelihood of confusion only the essential function, *i.e.* the origin function, was of relevance (para 59).

The additional trade mark functions have come to prominence in particular in the CJEU's AdWord cases. In its *Google France* decision[53] the Court, after summing up its jurisprudence regarding trade mark functions (paras. 75–79), goes on to examine not only the function of indicating origin but also, for the first time in more detail, the advertising function:

> Since the course of trade provides a varied offer of goods and services, the proprietor of a trade mark may have not only the objective of indicating, by means of that mark, the origin of its goods or services, but also that of using its mark for advertising purposes designed to inform and persuade consumers.

---

[52] Judgment of the CJEU of 18 June 2009, *L'Oréall v. Bellure*, C-487/07, ECLI:EU:C:2009/378.

[53] Judgment of the CJEU of 23 March 2010, *Google France*, joined cases C-236/08 to C-238/08, ECLI:EU:C:2010:159.

> Accordingly, the proprietor of a trade mark is entitled to prohibit a third party from using, without the proprietor's consent, [an identical trade mark for identical goods] where that use adversely affects the proprietor's use of its mark as a factor in sales promotion or as an instrument of commercial strategy. (paras. 91–92)

The Court then applies these principles to the facts of the case, *i.e.* the use of a third-party trade mark as an AdWord, in unusual detail:

> With regard to the use by internet advertisers of a sign identical with another person's trade mark as a keyword for the purposes of displaying advertising messages, it is clear that that use is liable to have certain repercussions on the advertising use of that mark by its proprietor and on the latter's commercial strategy.
>
> Having regard to the important position which internet advertising occupies in trade and commerce, it is plausible that the proprietor of a trade mark may register its own trade mark as a keyword with a referencing service provider in order to have an ad appear under the heading "sponsored links". [...] [e]ven if the proprietor of the mark is prepared to pay a higher price per click than that offered by third parties which have also selected that trade mark, the proprietor cannot be certain that its ad will appear before those of those third parties, given that other factors are also taken into account in determining the order in which the ads are displayed.
>
> Nevertheless, those repercussions of use by third parties of a sign identical with the trade mark do not of themselves constitute an adverse effect on the advertising function of the trade mark.
>
> [...] when internet users enter the name of a trade mark as a search term, the home and advertising page of the proprietor of that mark will appear in the list of the natural results, usually in one of the highest positions on that list. That display, which is, moreover, free of charge, means that the visibility to internet users of the goods or services of the proprietor of the trade mark is guaranteed, irrespective of whether or not that proprietor is successful in also securing the display, in one of the highest positions, of an ad under the heading "sponsored links". (paras. 93–97)

The Court concludes that the use of the claimant's trade mark by the defendant as an AdWord was not liable to have an adverse effect on the advertising function of the mark.

C. THE INVESTMENT FUNCTION

In another AdWord case (*Interflora*)[54] the CJEU confirmed its assessment of the effects of AdWord advertisements on the advertising function (and the function of indicating origin), but added comments on possible adverse effects of AdWords on the investment function:

[54] Judgment of the CJEU of 22 September 2011, *Interflora v. Marks & Spencer*, C-323/09, ECLI:EU:C:2011:604.

> In addition to its function of indicating origin and, as the case may be, its advertising function, a trade mark may also be used by its proprietor to acquire or preserve a reputation capable of attracting consumers and retaining their loyalty.
>
> Although that function of a trade mark – called the "investment function" – may overlap with the advertising function, it is none the less distinct from the latter. Indeed, when the trade mark is used to acquire or preserve a reputation, not only advertising is employed, but also various commercial techniques.
>
> When the use by a third party, such as a competitor of the trade mark proprietor, of [an identical sign for identical goods] substantially interferes with the proprietor's use of its trade mark to acquire or preserve a reputation capable of attracting consumers and retaining their loyalty, the third party's use must be regarded as adversely affecting the trade mark's investment function. The proprietor is, as a consequence, entitled to prevent such use [...].
>
> In a situation in which the trade mark already enjoys such a reputation, the investment function is adversely affected where use by a third party of a sign identical with that mark in relation to identical goods or services affects that reputation and thereby jeopardises its maintenance. As the Court has already held, the proprietor of a trade mark must be able, by virtue of the exclusive right conferred upon it by the mark, to prevent such use [...]. (paras. 60–63)

As with the advertising function, however, the Court goes on to narrow the protection given by the investment function considerably (at least in the case of AdWords):

> However, it cannot be accepted that the proprietor of a trade mark may – in conditions of fair competition that respect the trade mark's function as an indication of origin – prevent a competitor from using a sign identical with that trade mark in relation to goods or services identical with those for which the mark is registered, if the only consequence of that use is to oblige the proprietor of that trade mark to adapt its efforts to acquire or preserve a reputation capable of attracting consumers and retaining their loyalty. Likewise, the fact that that use may prompt some consumers to switch from goods or services bearing that trade mark cannot be successfully relied on by the proprietor of the mark. (para. 64)

D. THE QUALITY AND COMMUNICATION FUNCTIONS

The quality and communication functions have so far received less attention from the Court (and presumably the parties arguing before the Court). Advocate General Kokott has, however, made some comments on the quality and communication functions in her opinion in the 'Viking Gas' case.[55]

[55] Opinion of AG Kokott of 7 April 2011, *Viking Gas A/S v. Kosan Gas A/S*, C-46/10, ECLI:EU:C:2011:222.

Regarding the quality function AG Kokott notes that

> As a rule, the function of guaranteeing the quality of the goods goes hand in hand with the function of guaranteeing its origin. The trade mark indicates that the goods satisfy the quality standards of the recognisable proprietor of the trade mark. Therefore, as a rule, the function in relation to quality is adversely affected, if goods not attaining those quality requirements are commercialised under the trade mark, for example, by licensees or following impairment by the purchaser. (para. 45)

She goes on to point out, however, that

> cases also exist in which a trade mark indicates the quality of goods without referring to its specific origin. For example, an association of German mineral water companies is the proprietor of a collective trade mark in the form of a water bottle. That bottle is used by many companies and, thus, cannot indicate the origin of the water. However, it can only be used for mineral water and, thus, signalises that product characteristic. Accordingly, use in connection with table water would adversely affect the function through which quality is guaranteed. (para. 47)

In the case concerned (pertaining to the defendant's refilling of the claimant's gas bottles, the form of which is protected by 3D trade marks) AG Kokott nevertheless suggests denying claims of an impairment of the quality function on the grounds that

> there is nothing to suggest that the gas bottle is intended to guarantee a particular quality of gas which is, in that sense, independent of the origin of the gas. Moreover, the Commission emphasised the fact that bottled gas is a standardised product and, as a result, consumers expect, in general, the same quality of product from all providers. Thus, where there are adequate indications of the refilling company, there is nothing to suggest an adverse effect on the function by which quality is guaranteed. (paras. 48–49)

AG Kokott then turns to the other trade mark functions, noting that

> the commercialisation of refilled bottles could adversely affect the functions of the trade mark with respect to communication, investment and advertising. (para. 50)

She follows with some quite interesting observations on the connection between the different trade mark functions (paras 50 pp.). The immediate purpose of trade mark rights, AG Kokott notes, is to ensure exclusive use of the mark such that the proprietor may strengthen the connection between that sign and its goods and that that function of the trade mark is affected where others use the mark even if it is clarified in the context of such use that the goods are of a different origin. Consumers who have bought goods bearing that mark from a different company will associate them less readily with its proprietor. This constitutes a disadvantage for the trade mark owner which affects not only the advertising function but also the communication function and, indirectly, taking account of the costs of the licence for the trade mark, also the investment function. The fact that a bottle of a certain shape does not remain exclusively associated with the trade mark owner has implications for the bottle's significance as a trade mark and its use for publicity purposes.

AG Kokott then makes the interesting point that the disadvantage to the proprietor of the trade mark consists, ultimately, in the dilution of the mark against which, in principle, only marks with a reputation are protected and which, in addition, presupposes a use of the sign without due cause that takes unfair advantage of the distinctive character of the mark. She notes that, while 'simple trade marks' (*i.e.* trade marks that do not have a reputation) are protected, in principle, against dilution, that protection is nothing other than a reflex of the protection afforded to the function indicating origin, which is evident, AG Kokott points out, from the fact that 'simple trade marks' may be used by others for dissimilar goods and services, which is also susceptible to undermine the distinctive character of the mark.

Ultimately, AG Kokott concludes that none of the trade mark functions are impaired in the case concerned and recommends dismissing the claims of trade mark infringement (as the court subsequently did).

E. THE CURRENT STATUS OF THE CONCEPT OF TRADE MARK FUNCTIONS

The current status of the concept of trade mark functions is summed up in the CJEU's *Mitsubishi* decision[56] of 2018:

> The Court has held on many occasions that that exclusive right of the proprietor of the mark was conferred in order to enable him to protect his specific interests as proprietor, namely to ensure that the trade mark can fulfil its function, and that the exercise of that right must therefore be reserved to cases in which a third party's use of the sign affects, or is liable to affect, the functions of the trade mark [...].
>
> As regards those functions, it must be borne in mind that the <u>essential function</u> of a trade mark is to guarantee the <u>identity of the origin</u> of the marked goods or service to the consumer or end user by enabling him to distinguish the goods or service from

56 Judgment of the CJEU of 25 July 2018, *Mitsubishi v. Duma Forklifts*, C-129/17, ECLI:EU:C:2018:594.

> others which have another origin [...]. It serves in particular to guarantee that all the goods or services bearing it have been manufactured or supplied under the control of a single undertaking which is responsible for their quality, which it does in order to fulfil its essential role in the system of undistorted competition [...].
>
> The function of investment of the mark includes the possibility for the proprietor of a mark to employ it in order to acquire or preserve a reputation capable of attracting customers and retaining their loyalty, by means of various commercial techniques. Thus, when the use by a third party, such as a competitor of the trade mark proprietor, of a sign identical to the trade mark in relation to goods or services identical with those for which the mark is registered substantially interferes with the proprietor's use of its trade mark to acquire or preserve a reputation capable of attracting consumers and retaining their loyalty, the third party's use adversely affects that function of the trade mark. [...].
>
> As to the function of the advertising of the mark, it is that of using a mark for advertising purposes designed to inform and persuade consumers. Accordingly, the proprietor of a trade mark is, in particular, entitled to prohibit a third party from using, without the proprietor's consent, a sign identical with its trade mark in relation to goods or services which are identical with those for which that trade mark is registered, where that use adversely affects the proprietor's use of its mark as a factor in sales promotion or as an instrument of commercial strategy [...]. (paras. 34–37, emphasis added)

Thus, we have

- The function of indicating the origin; this is the 'essential' function of all trade marks;
- Additional functions that are only granted in cases of double identity, namely
  - The advertising function;
  - The investment function;
  - The quality function;
  - The communication function.

While the function of indicating origin, the advertising function and the investment function have been subject to further clarification as to their scope by the Court, the exact scope of the investment and quality functions is not yet clear.

A further point that is in need of clarification is the relationship between the advertising, investment, quality and communication functions as applied in the context of double identity cases (article 5(1)(a) TMD) and the special protection granted to well-known marks according to article 5(3) TMD (formerly article 5(2) TMD).

The CJEU has not yet explicitly addressed that question. It has, however, been discussed by AG Jääskinen in his opinion in 'Interflora'[57]:

> In the case of double identity it is possible to think that protection against blurring, tarnishment and free-riding would be based on Article 5(1)(a) only, and not involving Article 5(2) at all. This would be the case provided that the use of a sign identical with a trade mark in relation to identical goods or services would be liable to have an adverse effect on any of the functions of the trade mark. Here concerned would be most obviously the quality, communication, advertising or investment functions, but also the identification or distinguishing function in so far as the sign is used to distinguish between goods and services for purposes other than for indicating their origin.
>
> Such interpretation would be consistent with the idea expressed in the 10th recital in the preamble to Directive 89/104 according to which the protection provided by Article 5(1)(a) is 'absolute'. For me it is also obvious that any of the uses covered by Article 5(2) of Directive 89/104 are likely to have an adverse effect on at least some of the trade mark functions mentioned above, especially since the widened protection provided by Article 5(2) of Directive 89/104 is usually motivated with reference to the communication, advertising and investment functions of trade marks.
>
> This reasoning would entail that Article 5(1)(a) would protect against the forms of dilution mentioned in Article 5(2) in cases of double identity between signs and goods or services. Moreover, the distinctiveness and repute would in this case be protected irrespective of whether the trade mark has a reputation or not [...].
>
> Nevertheless, such an interpretation would contradict the letter though perhaps not the ratio decidendi of Davidoff. There the Court declared Article 5(2) of Directive 89/104 applicable not only in the case of similar goods but also in the case of identical goods, even if the reasoning put forward by the Court would seem to be relevant only with respect of the first mentioned situation.
>
> However, I would be reluctant to recommend the Court to answer question 3 along the lines that only Article 5(1)(a) of Directive 89/104 is applicable, especially since the Court already seems to have accepted parallel application of Article 5(1)(a) and (2) of Directive 89/104. [...] Whatever the merits of the role of the trade mark functions in the application of Article 5(1)(a) it seems to me that trade mark dilution as a legal phenomenon should in all cases be analysed on the basis of Article 5(2). This would entail that the notions relating to trade mark dilution are interpreted uniformly despite the differences in the degrees of similarity required to exist between allegedly infringing goods or services and those covered by a trade mark in the situations referred to in Article 5(1)(a), (1)(b) and (2) of Directive 89/104 respectively. Therefore in my opinion all trade mark functions – with the exception of the origin function – can have a role to play in the application of Article 5(2)

[57] Opinion of AG Jääskinen of 24 March 2011, *Interflora v. Marks & Spencer*, C-323/09, ECLI:EU:C:2011:173, paragraphs 60 to 64; see also AG Kokott's opinion of 7 April 2011, *Viking Gas A/S v. Kosan Gas A/S*, C-46/10, ECLI:EU:C:2011:222, already discussed above.

> of Directive 89/104 even if they have already been applied in determining the applicability of Article 5(1)(a).'

It remains to be seen how the Court will eventually resolve the overlap of article 5(1)(a) and (what is now) article 5(3) TMD.

4. THE RECEPTION OF THE SYSTEM OF TRADE MARK FUNCTIONS BY THE EUIPO

The EUIPO has picked up on the Court's jurisprudence pertaining to the different trade mark functions. As the concept of trade mark functions has been developed within the framework of infringement proceedings and the EUIPO is, obviously, not concerned with trade mark infringement, the context of the discussion of trade mark functions is – necessarily – different. The use the EUIPO has made of the concept of trade mark functions is nevertheless interesting.

For example, in its 'UNICORN' decision of 2015[58] the Fifth Board of Appeal has utilised the concept of different trade mark functions in its discussion of the protection conferred by article 8(5) CTMR (well-known marks):

> In order to better define the risk referred to in Article 8(5) CTMR, it must be pointed out that the primary function of a mark is unquestionably that of an "indication of origin" [...]. The fact remains that a mark also acts as a means of conveying other messages concerning, inter alia, the qualities or particular characteristics of the goods or services which it covers or the images and feelings which it conveys, such as luxury, lifestyle, exclusivity, adventure or youth, etc. To that effect, the mark has an inherent economic value which is independent of, and separate from, that of the goods and services for which it is registered. The messages in question which are conveyed by a mark with a reputation or which are associated with it confer on that mark a significant value which deserves protection, particularly because, in most cases, the reputation of a mark is the result of considerable effort and investment on the part of its proprietor. The Court has also recognised the advertising and investment function of a trade mark [...]. Consequently, Article 8(5) CTMR ensures that a mark with a reputation is protected with regard to any application for an identical or similar mark which might adversely affect its image, even if the goods or services covered by the mark applied for [...] are not similar to those for which the earlier mark with a reputation has been registered [...]. (para. 13)

---

58 Decision of the Fifth Board of Appeal of 16 February 2015 in case R 1699/2014–5 'UNICORN / UNICORN et al.'.

The same wording can be found in other Board of Appeal decisions.[59]

Thus, the EUIPO uses the concept of trade mark functions not to assess infringement but rather to define the scope of protection of well-known marks (article 8(5) EUTMR). It will be interesting to watch the direction the EUIPO is taking with this approach and whether the courts will have a chance to weigh in on it.

5. THE RECEPTION AND CRITICISM OF THE SYSTEM OF TRADE MARK FUNCTIONS AND PROPOSALS FOR A REFORM

While the concept of trade mark functions as developed by the CJEU has been greeted by some[60], it has also met with criticism.

One of the most prominent critics has been Lord Justice Jacob, delivering the opinion of the Court of Appeal (England and Wales) (Civil Division), in its judgment[61] following the CJEU's decision in case C-487/07 'L'Oréal'[62]:

> In [56] [the CJEU] appears to be explicitly saying that the use we have to consider is indeed within Art.5(1)(a); "Such use falls within the scope of application of Art. 5(1)(a)." One might have thought that was an end of the point. But then the Court then goes on to refer back to us, the question in [63]. We are to consider whether the functions of communication, investment or advertising are liable to be affected, even though the use "is not capable of jeopardising the essential function of the mark which is to indicate the origin of the goods. [65]
>
> I am bound to say that I have real difficulty with these functions when divorced from the origin function. There is nothing in the legislation about them. Conceptually they are vague and ill-defined. Take for instance the advertising and investment functions. Trade mark owners of famous marks will have spent a lot of money creating them and need to continue to spend to maintain them. But all advertisements for rival products will impinge on the owner's efforts and affect the advertising and investment function of the brand in question. No-one would say such jostling for fame and image in the market should be stopped. Similarly all comparative advertising (for instance that in O2 v Hutchinson [2008] ECR I-04231,

59 Cf. Decision of the Fifth Board of Appeal in case R 0779/2014-5 'SOLVO (FIG. MARK) / VOLVO' at para. 34 and Decision of the Second Board of Appeal in case R 1744/2014-2 'LEGARIS / LEGARIS et al.' at para. 28.

60 Cf. Fezer, Markenrecht, 4th ed., Einleitung Rn. 21 pp.; Fezer, GRUR 2003, 457.

61 L'Oréal SA & Ors v Bellure NV & Ors [2010] EWCA Civ 535 (21 May 2010) (paras. 29–32).

62 Judgment of the CJEU of 18 June 2009, *L'Oréall v. Bellure*, C-487/07, ECLI:EU:C:2009/378.

said to be acceptable by the Court) is likely to affect the value of the trade mark owner's investment.

So far as this case is concerned, however, it seems that the Court has indicated the answer as to whether the use is within Art. 5(1(a). According to the Court the use goes beyond "purely descriptive" use because it is used for advertising. A line is apparently to be drawn between something like a discussion between a would-be seller and his potential customer ("I can supply a diamond cut in the same shape as Spirit Sun"), which is apparently not "advertising" even though "Spirit Sun" is being used to gain a sale, and an out-and-out general purpose advertising aid such as a comparison list. I confess I do not know where that line is, but this case falls the wrong side of it. Why? Because the Court has said so. It regards the use as affecting the communication, advertising and investment functions of the mark.

I confess I regret that the same result was not achieved by a clearer direct route, namely to say simply that it was a case of same mark/same goods and that there is only an escape if Art. 6(1)(b) applies. I note that Arnold J is of the same view, see eBay at [292] and [306].'

There have been critics in academia, as well. Ohly has criticised the functions doctrine as a 'black box' with results that are hard to predict.[63] Kur has also been critical of the functions doctrine, noting that it leads to an 'unfortunate' structure of the assessment, with a very narrow and specific initial examination, which, in her opinion, would be better left to the statutory limitations.[64] She further criticizes the fact that the functions doctrine leads to cases being decided 'completely detached' from the letter of the law, based solely on an 'exegesis' of the trade mark functions.[65] Arnold has also sharply criticized the functions doctrine, noting in particular that it is not clear from the CJEU's case law what the functions doctrine adds to the requirement of 'use for goods and services' (*i.e.* 'use as a trade mark'), what the relationship is between article 10(2)(a) TMD and article 10(2)(c) TMD in double identity cases and that it is unclear who bears the burden of proof.[66]

The criticism of the functions doctrine, in particular its vagueness, has led the European Commission to propose in 2013 to explicitly state in the CTMR that the function of indicating the origin is the only (relevant) function when it comes to assessing infringement of trade marks.[67] The Commission's proposed wording for Recital 15 was:

63 GRUR 2011, 1131, 1132.

64 BeckOK, MarkenG, Einleitung Markenrecht, at paras. 146.

65 BeckOK, MarkenG, Einleitung Markenrecht, at paras. 148.1, citing as an example the CJEU's Judgment of 25 July 2018 in case C-129/17.

66 Arnold, GRUR Int. 2016, 884.

67 Proposal of the European Commission for an amended Regulation on the Community trade mark, https://eur-lex.europa.eu/legal-content/EN/TXT/?uri=CELEX%3A52013PC0161.

> In order to ensure legal certainty and clarity, it is necessary to clarify that not only in the case of similarity but also in case of an identical sign being used for identical goods or services, protection should be granted to a European trade mark **only if and to the extent that the main function** of the European trade mark, **which is to guarantee the commercial origin of the goods or services, is adversely affected.** (emphasis added)

The Commission further proposed amending article 9(2)(a) CTMR to read:

> [...] the proprietor of a European trade mark shall be entitled to prevent all third parties not having his consent from using in the course of trade any sign in relation to goods or services where:
>
> (a) the sign is identical with the European trade mark and is used in relation to goods or services which are identical with those for which the European trade mark is registered, **and where such use affects or is liable to affect the function of the European trade mark to guarantee to consumers the origin of the goods or services**' (emphasis added)

The Commission stated the following grounds for its proposal (on p. 8):

> The recognition of additional trade mark functions under Article 5(1)(a) of the Directive (Article 9(1)(a) of the Regulation) has created legal uncertainty. In particular, the relationship between double identity cases and the extended protection afforded by Article 5(2) of the Directive (Article 9(1)(c) of the Regulation) to trade marks having a reputation has become unclear. In the interest of legal certainty and consistency, it is clarified that in cases of both double identity under Article 9(1)(a) and similarity under Article 9(1)(b) it is only the origin function which matters.[68]

It is interesting to note that the Commission has not dismissed the relevance of trade mark function(s) in determining infringement under article 5(1)(a) CTMR outright (as suggested by some of the critics, notably Lord Justice Jacob), but has rather proposed to limit the assessment to the 'essential' function, *i.e.* the function of indicating origin.

The Commission's proposal has, however, been rejected by Parliament in the legislative process. In the legislative materials no justification is given. Whatever the reasons Parliament might have had, it seems unlikely that the Commission will make a new proposal to restrict the trade mark functions to the function of indicating origin after its proposal of 2013 was rejected.

68 For the perceived legal uncertainties created by the additional trade mark functions the Commission makes reference to AG Jääskinen's opinion in case C-323/09 'Interflora'.

6. THE FUTURE OF THE SYSTEM OF TRADE MARK FUNCTIONS

Where the CJEU and the national courts will take the system of trade mark functions in the coming years is hard to predict. One thing, however, seems sure: The doctrine of trade mark functions is here to stay.

It is to be hoped that the CJEU will have opportunities to further clarify the place of the functions doctrine in the assessment of trade mark infringement and in particular the scope of the various trade mark functions, as well as their relationship with the special protection granted to trade marks with a reputation.

IV. REFLECTIONS ON RECENT SWEDISH TRADEMARK CASE LAW IN LIGHT OF THE CJEU'S PRELIMINARY RULINGS

Richard WESSMAN, Stojan ARNERSTÅL
and Sofia BERGENSTRÅHLE

The purpose of this article is to celebrate the 25th anniversary of the community trademarks (now known as the EU trademarks) by providing some of our reflections on the most relevant Swedish trademark cases which have been subject to preliminary rulings. When a national court assigns questions of interpretation for preliminary rulings by the Court of Justice of the European Union (CJEU), in accordance with what is currently Article 267 TFEU, we are often only given a part of the CJEU's judgment as regards the abstract question of interpretation involved. This is a problem as we then often lack information about how the national court assesses and uses the preliminary ruling in the specific pending case at the national court. This information is often not as easily accessible as the CJEU's preliminary rulings[69], and in some cases there is of course also the problem that the judgment from the national court may only be available in the local language. We believe that we should all be better at bringing out and discussing the actual judgments of the national courts to increase the depth of understanding of what the outcome of the CJEU's preliminary ruling actually is, taking into account also the circumstances concerning the specific case. Hence, the purpose of this article is to provide such analysis in relation to the recent Swedish trademark case law which has been subject to preliminary rulings before being assessed by the national Swedish courts.

---

69 The CJEU's preliminary rulings are published and available online and are also translated to be accessible in the various languages of the EU member states.

1. RELEVANT SWEDISH CASE LAW

During the past quarter of a century, five Swedish trademark cases have been sent to the CJEU for preliminary rulings.[70] We have chosen to include the following three Swedish cases in our analysis:

1. The *Östgötatrafiken bus case*[71], see also the CJEU's preliminary ruling C-456/19, concerning the assessment of distinctive character for signs which are intended to be affixed to goods used to provide the service;
2. The *Svenskt Tenn case*[72], see also the CJEU's preliminary ruling C-21/18, regarding the interpretation of a "sign which consists exclusively of the shape" as an absolute ground for refusal, and;
3. The *Länsförsäkringar case*[73], see also the CJEU's preliminary ruling C-654/15, regarding the assessment of confusion when the trademark holder had not made "genuine use" of the trademark for the relevant goods and services within the stipulated five-year period.

2. THE ÖSTGÖTATRAFIKEN BUS CASE

A. BACKGROUND OF THE CASE

The public transport company Östgötatrafiken filed three applications for trademarks with the Swedish Patent and Registration Office (SPRO) for various services provided by means of vehicles and transport services. The applications were described as "Colouring of vehicles in the colours red, white and orange, as shown" (see some of the trademarks applied for below). The application did not, however, concern the actual shape of the vehicles or the black or grey colour covering that shape.

The SPRO rejected the applications on the basis that the signs were devoid of distinctive character. The SPRO explained that the signs were merely decorative and that they did not distinguish the services covered by the applications. The SPRO found that since commercial transport vehicles are often decorated with coloured motifs, the consumers must familiarise themselves with such elements before they perceive these elements as an indication of commercial origin.

---

70 See the following preliminary rulings: C-316/05, C-654/15, C-705/17, C-21/18 and C-456/19.

71 The PMCA's judgment dated 1 March 2021 in case no. PMÖÄ 3878-18.

72 The PMCA's judgment dated 16 March 2020 in case no. PMT 3491-16.

73 The Supreme Court's judgment dated 22 November 2017, referred to as NJA 2017 s. 905.

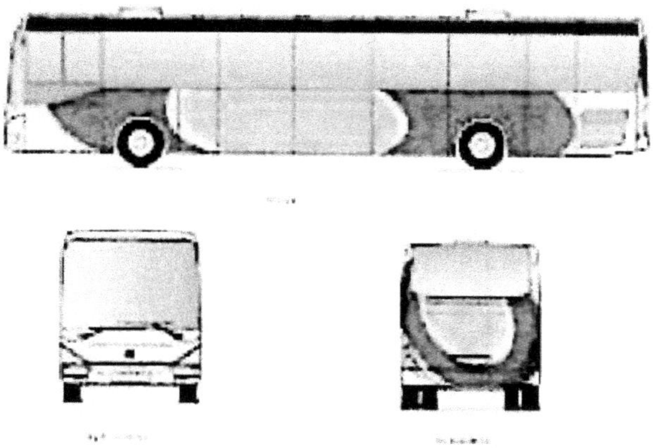

B. CJEU PRELIMINARY RULING

The Swedish Patent and Market Court of Appeal (PMCA) decided to submit the following questions to the CJEU for a preliminary ruling[74]:

> (1) Must Article 4(1)(b) of [Directive 2015/436] be interpreted as meaning that, in the case of an application for registration of a trademark which designates services and where the application relates to a sign, placed in a particular position, which covers large areas of the physical objects used to perform the services, it must be assessed whether the mark is not independent of the appearance of the objects concerned?
>
> (2) If the first question is answered in the affirmative, is it necessary for the trademark to depart significantly from the norm or customs of the economic sector concerned in order for the mark to be regarded as having distinctive character?[75]

According to Article 4(1)(b) of Directive 2015/436, an absolute ground for refusal or invalidity is when a trademark is devoid of any distinctive character. The CJEU concluded that "it follows from settled case-law that the essential function of a trademark is to ensure that the consumer or end user can identify the origin of the marked goods or services by enabling him or her, without any possibility of confusion, to distinguish the goods or services from others which have another origin"[76] and that in order to assess the distinctive character of a sign, an examination in the actual situation must be made where all the relevant

[74] C-456/19.
[75] C-456/19, paragraph 27.
[76] C-456/19, paragraph 32.

circumstances must be taken into consideration, including, when appropriate, the use of the sign.[77]

Furthermore, if the sign is intended to be affixed exclusively and systematically in a specific manner to large parts of the goods that are used to provide the service, the sign that is applied for to be a trademark cannot be assessed independently of the perception of the relevant public of the affixing of that sign on those goods, despite the fact that the trademark application does not include these goods, since the public perceives the sign as being affixed to the goods.[78]

The CJEU also stated that, when deciding if the sign has conferred inherent distinctive character, an overall analysis of the actual situation must be made of the systematically arranged colour combination. That condition is satisfied when the average consumer can distinguish, without any confusion, the transport services provided by an undertaking from those provided by other undertakings.[79] However, it is not necessary to examine if the signs for which registration as a trademark is sought depart significantly from the norm or customs of the economic sector concerned.[80]

C. SWEDISH JUDGMENT

Östgötatrafiken appealed the SPRO's decision to the Swedish Patent and Market Court (PMC).[81] In a judgment dated 29 March 2018, the PMC concluded that the placement of the filed trademarks on buses had such a strong connection to the transportation services for which trademarks were applied for that the trademark had to depart widely from the norm or the custom in the industry in order to be distinctive. The PMC ruled, much like the SPRO, that the signs were merely decorative. The PMC dismissed the action brought by Östgötatrafiken.

Östgötatrafiken appealed the judgment to the PMCA.[82] The court requested a preliminary ruling, as described above. Approximately five months after the preliminary ruling, the PMCA issued its judgment. The PMCA noted that the main question in this case was if the sign was *distinctive*. A sign must be distinctive in order to be a trademark according to Swedish law, which

77 C-456/19, paragraph 33.
78 C-456/19, paragraph 34–36.
79 C-456/19, paragraph 37.
80 C-456/19, paragraph 39.
81 PMÄ 14305-17, PMÄ 14437-17 and PMÄ 14453-17.
82 PMÖÄ 3878-18.

incorporates Article (3)(1)(b) of Directive 2008/95[83] (the previous trademark directive, which is identical with Article (4)(1)(b) in the new trademark directive, Directive 2015/2436[84]).

The PMCA held that, according to the CJEU, the distinctive character of the sign must be assessed in light of how the relevant public perceives the sign when applied on the buses and trains. The court thereafter made two separate assessments, since Östgötatrafiken applied for a trademark for two different categories; transportation of passengers and other goods and services with a close connection to these transportations.

In relation to the first category, the relevant public was, according to the court, consumers (both as private persons and businesses). The PMCA pointed out that not only the colours, but also the shape of the sign and the services for which the sign will be used for, must be taken into consideration when assessing whether a sign is distinctive. The PMCA pointed out that a sign that covers a larger part of an object is harder to perceive. However, the court also took into consideration that in everyday situations the relevant public view the buses and trains from a distance, which makes it easier to perceive the brand overall.

In this case, the PMCA found that figures made of asymmetrical ellipses with three contrasting colours indicated a commercial origin and that this was enough, without any possibility of confusion, to distinguish the transportation services provided by Östgötatrafiken from others which have another origin. The trademarks were thus distinctive in relation to the first category.

In relation to the second category and services with a close connection to the transportation of passengers and goods, the relevant public was the same as the one in the first category. The PMCA found that the trademarks were distinctive regarding most of the services, even though the sign marks on the actual buses and trains did not serve as a trademark function in this case. However, the PMCA called attention to the fact that pictures of buses and trains could be used when marketing these services. The PMCA concluded that the trademarks were distinctive regarding this category as well. Östgötatrafiken was also renting out buses and trains. Even though this service differed from the service of public transport, the PMCA found that the signs created a recollection about the origin of the service and therefore the signs affixed on the buses and trains worked as an indication of commercial origin.

83 Directive 2008/95/EC of the European Parliament and of the Council of 22 October 2008 to approximate the laws of the Member States relating to trade marks.

84 Directive (EU) 2015/2436 of the European Parliament and of the Council of 16 December 2015 to approximate the laws of the Member States relating to trade marks.

In summary, the PMCA ruled that all the signs had distinctive character regarding all the services, with the exception of the signs on the buses that did not have distinctive character regarding rail transport and *vice versa*.

D. CONCLUDING REMARKS

The CJEU concluded that signs which are intended to be affixed exclusively and systematically in a specific manner to large parts of the goods that are used to provide the service must not be assessed independently of the perception of the relevant public of the affixing of that sign on those goods. Instead, the distinctive character of the sign must be assessed in light of how the relevant public perceives the sign when applied on the relevant goods. However, it is not necessary to examine if the sign for which registration as a trademark is sought departs significantly from the norm or customs of the economic sector concerned. Hence, in the national case we are concerned with the PMCA made its assessment based on how the relevant public perceived the signs on buses and trains and thereby came to the conclusion that such affixed signs fulfilled the function of a trademark i.e. to indicate commercial origin. It cannot be ruled out that the outcome of the PMCA's assessment would have been different if the CJEU had e.g. advocated an assessment of the sign separated from the goods used to provide the service or had proclaimed that the court must also assess whether or not the signs in question departed from customs for signs used in public transport etc.

3. THE SVENSKT TENN CASE

A. BACKGROUND OF THE CASE

The limited company Svenskt Tenn (Svenskt Tenn) manufactures, markets and sells furniture, textiles and other interior fixtures and fittings. The company was founded in the 1920s. During the early 1930s, Svenskt Tenn initiated a collaboration with the architect Josef Frank and shortly thereafter Svenskt Tenn engaged him to design furniture and textiles. Josef Frank was from Austria, where he had his own business. He became a Swedish citizen in 1939. During the years 1941–1946, he lived in the U.S. Josef Frank passed away in 1967.

Josef Frank designed various patterns before and during his employment at Svenskt Tenn, patterns which to this day are being marketed by Svenskt Tenn. Svenskt Tenn holds the copyright to these designs. Svenskt Tenn holds the EU trademark JOSEF FRANK, a word mark, for i.e. fabrics, pillows and furniture.

The company also holds the EU trademark MANHATTAN, a figurative mark protecting the well-known pattern (see below), for textile products, etc.

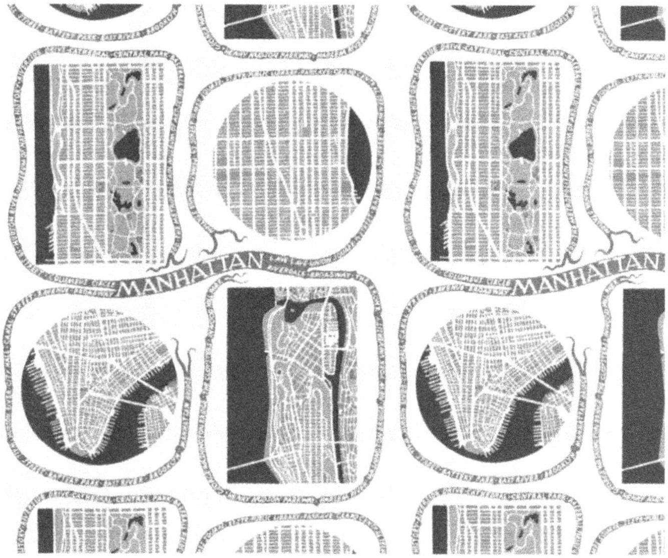

Textilis Ltd (Textilis) is an English company which sells fabrics and related products, without any intellectual property protection. The online company was marketing fabrics and goods bearing patterns which are similar to those of the figurative mark for which Svenskt Tenn is the proprietor of the trademark in question.

B. CJEU PRELIMINARY RULING

The PMCA requested a preliminary ruling[85] from the CJEU and wanted to clarify the interpretation of Article 7(1)(e)(iii) of Regulation 207/2009[86]; more specifically, the PMCA wanted to know if the article is applicable to a court's assessment of invalidity that is made after the entry into force of the amendment even if the declaration of invalidity was brought before the entry into force, and thus concerns a trademark registered before the date. The PMCA also wanted clarity regarding the scope of the article and whether it covers two-dimensional representation of a two dimensional product, for example fabric decorated with the sign in question and also regarding how the wording "signs which consist

[85] C-21/18.

[86] Council Regulation (EC) No 207/2009 of 26 February 2009 on the Community trade mark, hereinafter "Regulation 207/2009".

exclusively of the shape (or another characteristic) which gives substantial value to the goods" should be interpreted, in a situation where the registration covers a wide range of classes of goods and the sign may be affixed in different ways to the goods.[87]

Regarding the first question, the court stated that it follows from settled case-law that, in order to ensure legal certainty and protection of legitimate expectations, the substantive rules of EU law are only applicable to situations existing before their entry into force if it clearly follows from their terms, objectives or general scheme that the law has such an effect.[88] The directive did not have such a provision, and it did not follow from the purpose nor the scheme.[89] The CJEU therefore answered that the article must be interpreted as not being applicable to marks registered before the entry into force of the regulation.[90]

According to Article 7(1)(e)(iii) of Regulation 207/2009, a sign which consists exclusively of a shape which results from the nature of the goods themselves shall not be registered. The PMCA wanted clarity on how to interpret "exclusively of the shape" and if a sign, consisting of two-dimensional decorative motifs, which is affixed to products, such as fabric or paper, falls within the meaning of that provision.

The CJEU held that the meaning and scope of the concept of "shape" must be determined by considering its usual meaning in everyday language, while also taking into account the context in which it occurs and the purposes of the rules.[91] In the context of trademark law, it is usually understood as a set of lines or contours that outline the product concerned.[92] Even though the sign under consideration (MANHATTAN) represented a shape, formed by an external outline, the sign contains decorative elements inside and outside those lines, and additionally the sign highlights words.[93] Furthermore, the CJEU stated that "it cannot be held that a sign consisting of two-dimensional decorative motifs is indissociable from the shape of the goods where that sign is affixed to goods, such as fabric or paper, the form of which differs from those decorative motifs."[94] Therefore, a sign such as "MANHATTAN", which consists of a two-dimensional decorative motif, which is affixed to goods, such as fabric or paper, does not

87 C-21/18, paragraph 28.
88 C-21/18, paragraph 30.
89 C-21/18, paragraph 31–32.
90 C-21/18, paragraph 33.
91 C-21/18, paragraph. 35.
92 C-21/18, paragraph 36.
93 C-21/18, paragraph 40–41.
94 C-21/18, paragraph 42.

"consist exclusively" of the shape, within the meaning of Article 7(1)(e)(iii) of Regulation 207/2009.[95]

C. SWEDISH JUDGMENT

As mentioned above, Textilis marketed fabrics and goods for interior design bearing similar patterns to marks held by Svenskt Tenn, such as MANHATTAN. Svenskt Tenn thus brought an action for infringement. In response thereto, Textilis counterclaimed that the trademark was invalid, firstly because it lacked distinctive character and secondly because it is made up of a shape which gives substantial value to the goods, within the scope of Article 7(1)(e)(iii) of Regulation 207/2009.

The Stockholm District Court (District Court) dismissed the counterclaim. The trademark MANHATTAN as well as JOSEF FRANK had, according to the District Court, distinctive character. Textilis appealed this judgement to the PMCA. After the preliminary ruling, the PMCA issued a judgment dismissing Textilis' claim. First, the PMCA concluded that the patterns made by Josef Frank were subject to copyright since they are original and can be identified in a manner which makes them identifiable with sufficient precision and objectivity, and they can be referred to as "work" in accordance with Directive 2001/29.[96] Since Textilis was distributing products with these patterns to the public in Sweden, Textilis had violated Svenskt Tenn's copyright for the purposes of Article 4(1) of Directive 2001/29.

As regards the trademark MANHATTAN, Textilis claimed that the trademark lacked distinctive character and that it was a sign which exclusively consisted of a shape which results from the nature of the goods according to Article 7(1)(e)(iii) of Regulation 207/2009 and was thus invalid. As mentioned above, the CJEU stated that MANHATTAN represents a "shape" formed by an external outline, but it also has decorative elements. Furthermore, words are highlighted. Since the CJEU clearly stated that the sign MANHATTAN, which consists of a two-dimensional decorative motif, which is affixed to goods, such as fabric or paper, did not exclusively consist of a shape within the meaning of the article, there was no ground for refusal of trademark registration. There was no evidence which showed that the trademark lacked distinctive character. Textilis had wrongfully been using the trademarks JOSEF FRANK and MANHATTAN and had thus committed an infringement of the EU trademarks held by Svenskt Tenn.

---

95 C-21/18, paragraph 46.

96 Directive 2001/29/EC of the European Parliament and of the Council of 22 May 2001 on the harmonization of certain aspects of copyright and related rights in the information society.

D. CONCLUDING REMARKS

Signs which consist of two-dimensional decorative motifs, which are affixed to goods, such as fabric or paper, do not "consist exclusively" of the shape, within the meaning of Article 7(1)(e)(iii) of Regulation 207/2009 and can thereby be protected as a trademark should all other requirements be fulfilled. To conclude, the CJEU has clarified that there are no absolute grounds for refusal of registration of such signs. In the national case we are concerned with, the CJEU's clarification was of direct importance to the outcome of the case. Textilis' counterclaim – that the MANHATTAN trademark was invalid as it consisted exclusively of the shape – could obviously not be successful. The PMCA's assessment was in line with the CJEU's clarification in this regard.

4. THE LÄNSFÖRSÄKRINGAR CASE

A. BACKGROUND OF THE CASE

The Swedish limited company Länsförsäkringar operates in the fields of banking, investment and insurance. Länsförsäkringar is the proprietor of an EU figurative trademark, registered on 4 January 2008. Matek A/S (Matek) manufactures and assembles wooden houses. In 2007, Matek began to use a logo, which has been registered since 2009. Länsförsäkringar took the view that Matek, by using this logo, infringed the exclusive right conferred by the EU trademark of which it is the proprietor. However, Länsförsäkringar had not made genuine use of the EU trademark.

See below Länsförsäkringar's registered figurative trademark in black and white, and in colour.[97]

[97] Please note that since the Länsförsäkringar case, the PMCA has clarified that the trademark protection in Sweden shall be assessed using the "what you see is what you get" approach (instead of the "black and white covers all" approach), which means that a trademark filed in black and white is only protected as such. See the PMCA's decision dated 27 February 2019 in case number PMÖÄ 435-18 and the following article: https://www.lexology.com/library/detail.aspx?g=a122eaa0-49c2-4146-ab74-0eadc5d8b44c.

Figurative marks used by Matek (below).

B. CJEU PRELIMINARY RULING

The proprietor of an EU trademark has an exclusive right to the trademark. According to Article 9(1)(b) of Regulation 207/2009 (see the same article of Regulation 2017/1001), the proprietor is entitled to prevent all third parties not having his consent from using, in the course of trade, any sign where, because of its identity with, or similarity to, the EU trademark and the identity or similarity of the goods or services covered by the trademark and sign, there exists a likelihood of confusion on the part of the public; the likelihood of confusion includes the likelihood of association between the sign and the trademark.

Article 15(1) of Regulation 207/2009[98] states that the proprietor of a trademark must put the EU trademark to genuine use in the EU in connection with the goods or services which it is registered for within a period of five years following the registration. If the trademark proprietor does not do so, sanctions can be invoked. Article 51 of Regulation 207/2009 states that the rights shall be revoked if the trademark has not been put to genuine use within a continuous period of five years (Article 51(1)(a)). Article 51(2) states that, when the grounds for revocation of rights exist in respect of only some of the goods or services for which a trademark is registered, the rights shall be declared to be revoked in respect of those goods or services only.

The Swedish Supreme Court asked the CJEU if the exclusive rights conferred to an EU trademark according to Article 9(1)(b) of Regulation 207/2009 are affected when the proprietor has not made genuine use of the EU trademark in the EU for goods or services covered by the registration.[99] The CJEU stated that it follows from the wording and the purpose of Article 15(1), Article 15(1) and Article 51(1) and (2) of Regulation 207/2009 that the rights of the proprietor

[98] See article 18 of Regulation 2017/1001.
[99] C-654/15, paragraph 17.

cannot be declared to be revoked until the period of five years following the registration has expired.[100]

When determining whether the goods or services of the alleged infringer are identical or similar to the goods or services covered by the EU trademark concerned, the extent of the exclusive right should be assessed, during this period of five years, by having regard to the goods and services as covered by the trademark's registration.[101] Finally, the CJEU also stated that, when those five years have expired, the extent of that exclusive right may be affected by the fact that the proprietor has not begun genuine use of his trademark in response to some or all the goods and services which it has been registered for.[102]

C. SWEDISH JUDGMENT

Länsförsäkringar applied to the District Court on the basis of Article 9(1)(b) of Regulation 207/2009. Länsförsäkringar asserted that Matek, by using a logo similar to the one held by Länsförsäkringar, had infringed Länsförsäkringar's exclusive right. The District Court granted the application. The Svea Court of Appeal (Court of Appeal) set that decision aside. The Court of Appeal held that the examination of the goods and services at issue had to be made on the basis of the activity *actually carried out by the proprietor*, not the formal registration. Therefore, there was no likelihood of confusion.

Länsförsäkringar appealed to the Supreme Court. The Supreme Court pointed out that the CJEU in the preliminary ruling had held that there is an exclusive right conferred to an EU trademark during a period of five years, even if there is no genuine use.[103] The Supreme Court first examined whether there was a likelihood of confusion. While performing this examination, the Supreme Court held that it approached the trademark *as if* there was a genuine use.[104] In this scenario, there was a visual similarity between the trademark held by Länsförsäkringar and the one used by Matek. When Matek used their trademark with the text "matek TIMBER FRAME HOUSE", the similarity was reduced. Both Länsförsäkringar and Matek were marketing services related to buildings.[105]

100 C-654/15, paragraph 26.
101 C-654/15, paragraph 27.
102 C-654/15, paragraph 28.
103 NJA 2017 s. 905, paragraph 17.
104 NJA 2017 s. 905, paragraph 19.
105 NJA 2017 s. 905, paragraph 23.

However, Matek focused its business activities on professional operators, mostly dealers, architects and construction companies. They were mainly producing pre-fabricated houses for rent, schools and some private houses. Their marketing was targeting dealers, even though they were sometimes contacted by private individuals (the relevant public).[106] The Supreme Court held that professionals have good knowledge about trademarks in the industry, and that a purchase such as a pre-fabricated house is an important and expensive purchase for an individual, who therefore probably makes well informed and carefully weighed purchases. Accordingly, the Supreme Court took the view that there was no likelihood of confusion.[107] There was no infringement, and nor was Länsförsäkringar's reputation affected; see Article 9(1)(c) of Regulation 207/2009 (Article 9(2)(c) of Regulation 2017/1001).

D. CONCLUDING REMARKS

In the Länsförsäkringar case, the CJEU's response was unfortunately narrowly focused on the fact that during the first five-year period the goods and services that the registration formally refers to cannot be disregarded. The holder must therefore have the right to prevent third parties from using an identical or similar sign in respect of all goods and services which are identical or similar to those covered by the registration of the trademark. As regards whether this could lead to confusion among the public the CJEU's reply was diluted in that it only concerns the similarity assessment to be made for goods and services, not the later stage in the overall assessment. Thus, the CJEU largely avoided the interesting issue at stake for the national courts i.e. if it may be taken into account that that the sign has not been used during the first five-year period in the overall assessment to be carried out as regards the risk of confusion.

It can be noted that the CJEU's preliminary ruling itself indicated that Länsförsäkringar's claim against Matek would be successful when assessed by the national court, as it was clarified that a trademark proprietor may, during the period of five years following registration, prevent third parties from using identical or similar marks in respect of all goods and services covered by the registration without having to demonstrate genuine use of the mark in respect of those goods or services. When assessing the similarities between Länsförsäkringar and Matek's marks, the Supreme Court compared the relevant goods and services covered by Länsförsäkringar's registration with

106 NJA 2017 s. 905, paragraph 24.
107 NJA 2017 s. 905, paragraph 26.

the goods and services that Matek had undisputedly used its sign for. Even so, taking into account all the relevant circumstances of the similarity of the marks, goods and services, distinctive character and purchasing scenarios, the Supreme Court found that there was no likelihood of confusion. To conclude, the preliminary ruling did not affect the outcome in the national court in favour of the proprietor.

V. ENFORCEMENT OF UNREGISTERED RIGHTS AGAINST EU TRADE MARKS: DOES NATIONAL LAW ALWAYS PREVAIL?

Eva LACHMANNOVA

Throughout the whole existence of the Community and later European Union trade mark system, the Community (European Union) trade mark regulation has in its Article 8(4) provided for the possibility to oppose registration of a European trade mark (EUTM) based on an earlier national right to an unregistered trade mark. Owners of non-registered trade marks or of other signs used in the course of trade of more than mere local significance may enforce their rights against EUTM applications if, where and to the extent that pursuant to EU legislation or the law of the Member State governing that sign, rights to that sign were acquired prior to the date of application for registration of the EU trade mark, or the date of the priority claimed for the application for registration of the EU trade mark, and that sign confers on its proprietor the right to prohibit the use of a subsequent trade mark.

The European landscape of protection of unregistered signs is very diversified and the aim of this article is not to provide an exhaustive analysis of each national regime, but to identify gaps yet to be filled in the European practice based on my experience with my own national legal system, namely trade mark and unfair competition law in the Czech Republic. The discussion however touches principles common to other Member States and, as outlined in more detail below, similar issues have arisen in the past, at least in relation to France, Italy, Spain or Portugal.

1. FOUR CONDITIONS

In order to qualify for protection against earlier trade mark application by virtue of Article 8 (4) EUTMR, the non-registered trade mark or other sign must satisfy four conditions: (i) it must be used in the course of trade; (ii) it must be of more than mere local significance; (iii) the right to that mark or sign must have been acquired in accordance with EU law or the law of the Member State in which it was used prior to the date of application for registration of the EU trade mark; and (iv) the sign must confer on its proprietor the right to prohibit the use of a subsequent trade mark. The four conditions are cumulative: where a non-registered trade mark or a sign does not satisfy one of those conditions, the opposition cannot succeed.[108]

The first two conditions, requiring that the sign is used in the course of trade and that it is of a more than local significance are rooted directly in the provision of Article 8(4) and, as such, belong within the auspices of European law. Therefore, they need to be interpreted in a uniform way, regardless of the origin of the relevant unregistered mark or other sign. The European Union Intellectual Property Office (EUIPO) and the European courts will thus treat the issue of the scope of these conditions as a question of law.

On the other hand, the third and fourth conditions, namely the acquisition of rights to that sign prior to the date of application or priority and the existence of a right to prohibit the use of a subsequent mark are governed by the respective national law. This is where national law comes into play.

2. NATIONAL LAW AND OTHER QUESTIONS OF FACT

Questions related to the contents of the relevant national law applicable by virtue of Article 8 (4) are treated as questions of fact. Consequently, the applicant need not only prove that he satisfies the necessary conditions under the relevant national law which he seeks to apply, but also the particulars establishing the content of that law.[109]

According to Article 7 (2) (d) EUTMDR the opponent needs to provide in particular evidence showing use of that right in the course of trade of more than mere local significance, as well as evidence of its acquisition, continued existence and scope of protection (i.e. particulars relating to the first two conditions)

108 Judgment of the General Court of 12 October 2017, *Moravia Consulting v. EUIPO* – Citizen Systems Europe (SDC-888TII RU), T-317/16, not published, EU:T:2017:718, paragraph 38 and the case-law cited.

109 Judgments of the CJEU of 5 July 2011, Edwin v OHIM, C-263/09 P, EU:C:2011:452, paragraphs 49 and 50; of 27 March 2014, *OHIM v. National Lottery Commission*, C-530/12 P, EU:C:2014:186, paragraph 34; and of 5 April 2017, EUIPO v Szajner, C-598/14 P, EU:C:2017:265, paragraph 35.

and, where the earlier right is invoked pursuant to the law of a Member State, a clear identification of the content of the national law relied upon by adducing publications of the relevant provisions or jurisprudence (i.e. particulars relating to the third and fourth conditions).

EUIPO Guidelines and the practice of the General Court provide a detailed guidance on the issues to be proven, documents to be presented and the burden of proof as regards individual particulars.

According to the practice of the Court of Justice (CJEU), the opponent must establish that the sign concerned falls within the scope of the law of the Member State relied on and that it allows use of a subsequent mark to be prohibited. This requires, firstly, a finding that under the applicable law, rights of the type involved, in the abstract, are exclusive rights enforceable by means of an injunction vis-à-vis later marks and, secondly, a finding that in the actual case under consideration the conditions for obtaining such injunctive relief, if the mark that is the subject of the opposed EUTM application were used in the territory in question, are present (scope of protection). However, the opponent must establish only that he has available to him a right to prohibit use of a subsequent trade mark, but he cannot be required to establish that that right has been used, in other words that the opponent has actually been able to prohibit such use.[110]

Previous wording of EUIPO Guidelines provided applicants help in the form of an annex listing rights that (according to EUIPO's opinion) fall within the scope of rights under Article 8 (4) in individual Member States. Nevertheless, inclusion of the right to the annex had not precluded parties from providing evidence that the information contained in the list or otherwise established by the EUIPO is not correct or up to date.

On first sight, identifying and presenting relevant legal publications and copies of relevant court decisions seems an easy task for a trade mark professional, all the more so if you come from a country where protection of unregistered signs against confusion or parasitism has a long tradition.

3. UNREGISTERED SIGNS BASED ON CZECH LAW

As far as the Czech Republic is concerned, the 2017 edition of the EUIPO Guidelines listed in its Annex the provision of Section 7(1)(g) of the Czech Trademark Act, which reads in the relevant part:

---

110 Judgment of the CJEU of 29 March 2011, *Anheuser-Busch v. Budejovicky Budvar*-OHIM, C-96/09 P, paragraph 190 et seq.

The sign applied for shall not be included in the register upon opposition to the registration of the mark in the register ("the opposition") filed with the Office by

...

(g) the proprietor of a non-registered sign or of another sign used in the course of trade of more than mere local significance for identical or similar goods and services, if such sign is identical or similar to the sign applied for, if the rights to that sign were acquired prior to the date of the application for registration.[111]

As is apparent from the wording, this provision sets forth a relative ground of refusal of a national trade mark application based on the opposition filed by the proprietor of a non-registered sign or other sign that meets the conditions stipulated therein. The provision therefore clearly gives the user of such a sign the right to prevent registration of the trade mark.

Does this provision however entitle such a user to file a claim with the court seeking an injunction prohibiting use of the mark, the registration of which he is entitled to prevent? I believe that the answer to this question is not crystal clear, in spite of the fact that this question has repeatedly been answered in the affirmative by the EUIPO in several matters starting with the *GLADIATOR* case,[112] with a later confirmation of this approach by the General Court.

The General Court dealt with unregistered trade marks originating in the Czech Republic in the case involving an opposition filed by a Czech distillery Palírna U Zeleného stromu a.s. (formerly Granette & Starorežná Distilleries a.s.) against registration of a figurative sign 42 BELOW by Bacardi Co. Ltd, among others based on previous use of an unregistered figurative sign 42 VODKA.[113]

After being unsuccessful in the first instance, the opposition based on the earlier unregistered sign was upheld by the Board of Appeal. Bacardi contested the appellate decision based in particular on infringement of Article 8(4) of CTMR, putting forward among others the argument that the Board of Appeal did not carry out an exhaustive examination of the Czech law. According to Bacardi, the provision of Article 7(1)(g) of the Trademark Act was irrelevant, and the opposition should have been assessed in the light of provisions on unfair competition, at that time being Article 44 et seq. of the Commercial Code, which had been initially presented as the basis of the opposition by the opponent.[114]

---

111 Act no. 441/2003 Sb., Trademark Act.

112 Decision of the First Board of Appeal of EUIPO of 17 March 2011, R 1529/2010-1, GLADIATOR / GLADIATOR.

113 Judgment of the General Court of 24 October 2018, *Bacardi C. Ltd v EUIPO, 42 BELOW.*

114 Presently, unfair competition is governed by Article 2976 et seq. of the Czech Civil Code.

The General Court examined the scope of protection conferred to an unregistered mark by Article 7(1)(g) of the Trademark Act and firstly noted that, based on its literal wording, this Article expressly enshrines the right to oppose the registration of a later mark and that such protection is conditional on the unregistered sign's use in the course of trade.[115]

However, the General Court went on to infer that "by opposing the registration of a subsequent mark, the proprietors of rights over earlier signs seek effective protection against any future use of that mark" and concluded that "(...) Article 7(1)(g) of the Czech Law on trade marks enables the holder of a valid prior right to challenge a trade mark application before its registration, rather than having to go to court to have the use of the mark declared illegal and have the trade mark cancelled under Article 31(2) of that law. The right to oppose the registration of a subsequent mark under Article 7(1)(g) of the Czech Law on trade marks implicitly but necessarily includes the right to oppose the use of that mark."[116]

With respect to the provisions regulating unfair competition, the General Court found that the evidence adduced by the parties could not show that the Board of Appeal had erred in finding that those articles related to questions outside the sphere of competence of the EUIPO.

The judgment has however in my opinion not provided an exhaustive answer to the plea raised by Bacardi.

4. QUESTIONS RAISED BY THE BACARDI JUDGMENT

According to the well-established principle and one of the basic constitutional rights granted by the Czech legal system, anyone may do what is not prohibited by law, and no one may be forced to do what the law does not require.

Within the business and intellectual property domain, this freedom is limited by Article 8 of the Czech Trademark Act, providing the owner of a trade mark in line with the European trade marks Directive with the exclusive right to use it in the course of trade in relation to the goods and services for which it is protected. In its paragraph 2, the article prohibits anyone from using signs in cases of

115 *42 BELOW*, paragraph 98 and 99.
116 *42 BELOW.*

double identity, likelihood of confusion and situations falling within the scope of protection of trade marks with reputation.

The group of trade marks enjoying protection in the territory of the Czech Republic is defined in Article 3 of the Czech Trademarks Act, listing registered national trade marks, International Registrations, EUTMs, and well-known trade marks pursuant to Article 6 *bis* of the Paris Convention.

Nothing in these two articles prohibits the use in the course of trade of a sign identical with or similar to a sign that has not been registered as a trade mark, unless it can qualify as a well-known trade mark under Article 6 *bis* of the Paris Convention. At the same time, there is no other provision in the Trademark Act that would include a rule to that effect.

The right to seek an injunction against the use of an earlier mark based on trade mark protection is (and was at the time of the filing of the 42 BELOW application) set forth not in the Czech Trademark Act, but in the Act on Enforcement of Industrial Property Rights, namely its Article 4, implementing the relevant provisions of the Enforcement Directive and listing remedies available in the case of an infringement of an industrial property right, including trade mark infringement. Again, there is nothing in this act that would suggest that it could be used to obtain an injunction based on the rights to an unregistered sign.

On the other hand, provisions allowing businesses to seek protection of their unregistered signs may very easily be found in the legislation governing unfair competition – presently the Civil Code and formerly, until 31 December 2011, the above referenced provisions of the Commercial Code. Although the wording of the relevant provisions has changed with the switch to the Civil Code, it suffices for the purposes of this article to mention that the protection against unfair competition has been based on a general clause similar to the one included in the Paris Convention, making protection conditional upon the act being contrary to honest practices of competition and the potential of the act to harm competitors and/or consumers. Typical trade mark-related unfair practices, such as deceptive marking of goods, creating a danger of confusion or parasitism, among others, are specifically prohibited, with the elements of creating a danger of confusion being very similar to those provisions protecting trade marks against likelihood of confusion, but being available to any rightful user of a sign in the course of trade.

For an act to qualify as an act of unfair competition, the elements of the general clause must always be met. Therefore, although the elements that need to be proven in order to establish confusion as an act of unfair competition are mostly very similar to a trade mark infringement claim, the claimant seeking an injunction based on unfair competition must also successfully deal with the elements of the general clause. This creates some, albeit in practice quite tiny, room for escape in complex situations such as those involving long-term coexistence. Also, as a rule, the whole context of use of the earlier sign such as the appearance of the whole product, are taken into consideration.

Reading through the relevant provisions of the Czech law again it seems difficult to agree with the general conclusion made by both the EUIPO and the General Court that Article 7(1)(g) implicitly establishes the prohibition for third parties to use such a sign and a corresponding right of a user of an unregistered right to seek a court injunction ordering such third parties to cease and desist from such use without further ado. This general conclusion tends to extend the legal monopoly and absolute right granted to owners of registered trade marks beyond the scope expressly defined by law.

I am not aware of and have not been able to identify any published Czech case law where an injunction would be granted for the protection of an unregistered sign (leaving aside well-known trade marks) that would be based on Article 7(1)(g) of the Czech Trademark Act. On the contrary, such injunctions are available and granted by the courts based on the provisions on unfair competition. The factual finding of the General Court therefore seems at least somewhat incomplete, although room must be reserved for clarification based on the contents of the evidence materials on file, to which I do not have full access.

One may perhaps ask whether the General Court in fact meant to extend the scope of opposable right under Article 8(4) to any right that may prevent registration of an identical or similar sign as a trade mark, and thus prevent the obtaining of a legal monopoly for use and the right to prevent others from using such a sign by another. The same effect could also be achieved if the European instances openly interpreted the wording of Article 8(4) by finding that the fourth condition of its applicability encompasses not only the availability of injunction against use, but also a potential to prevent registration of an earlier sign based on the relevant national law.

This approach involves an extensive interpretation of European law, but not a potentially questionable finding of fact, and is openly advocated by the relevant part of the EUIPO Manual.[117] On the other hand, one may argue that being able

117 Part 3.5.1.

to prevent others from registering a trade mark while leaving them free to use the sign, unless they violate another legal rule, is not the same as being able to prevent the very use of the sign. To me, the latter right seems to present a weapon too strong to be forged from the former merely by argumentum *a fortiori.*

5. ANSWERS FROM ELSEWHERE?

A final solution cannot in my opinion be found by comparison with the case law of the CJEU in matters involving the law of other Member States. Although similar findings can be traced in the LAGIOULE judgment case where, against the background of French law, this interpretation was presented as undisputed, this conclusion is presented as a finding of fact.[118]

In the judgment of the CJEU in *PALLADIUM PALACE IBIZA RESORT & SPA* issued one year after the General Court's judgment in *LAGIOULE* but before the one in *42 BELOW*, the CJEU held in a case involving a Spanish trade name the that Article 8(4) must be understood as encompassing the situation in which the owner of a sign is, by virtue of the applicable national law, in a position to prevent such use by means of an invalidity action against a more recent mark. However, if we come back to the Czech environment, it is commonly the case that a successful opposition or invalidity action has in itself no impact on the legality of use of the earlier mark; therefore we cannot conclude that by virtue of the national law, the user of the unregistered sign would be in the position as described by the CJEU.

From my point of view, no satisfactory guidelines can be found in the *CARLO RONCATO* judgment involving a case based on the provisions of the Italian Industrial Property Code prohibiting registration of earlier marks under specific circumstances without any detailed reasoning as to the potential availability of an injunction under the same circumstances either.[119]

The Board of Appeal has also found Portuguese rules prohibiting registration of a subsequent mark based on business or corporate names and other distinctive signs to fall under the scope of Article 8 (4) EUTMR,[120] but this conclusion had not been tested at the General Court at the relevant time.

---

118 Judgment of the CJEU of 5 April 2017, *EUIPO v Szajner*, C-598/14 P, EU:C:2017:265, paragraph 37.

119 Judgment of the General Court of 7 July 2010, T-124/09, *Carlo Roncato*, EU:T:2010:290.

120 Decision of the Second Board of Appeal of EUIPO of 3 June 17/012015, R 2216/2014-2, *Sonicell (fig.) / SONICEL* et al.

6. CONCLUSION

With the above in mind, the *42 BELOW* judgment and the EUIPO case law on opposition based on unregistered signs under Article 8(4) EUTMR do in my opinion still leave room for future adjustments of the practice based on a more precise reflection of the relevant provisions of national law. Such adjustment or even change, if any, and any future attempts to prevail against an opposition based on a Czech unregistered right with a reference to an unfair competition defence, will certainly require a detailed argumentation and in particular the gathering of persuasive evidence of national law by the parties.

On a more general level, future oppositions or invalidation cases based on unregistered rights granted by the Czech law promise to present a fertile environment for further debates on the interplay between the European and national intellectual property systems or on the boundaries of interpretation of national law by the European institutions.

VI. THE EVOLUTION OF THE CONCEPT OF BAD FAITH UNDER EU TRADEMARK LAW

Diégo NOESEN

A trade mark can be refused or declared invalid if it was applied for in bad faith. This has always been an elusive concept, probably due to its subjective nature. After briefly addressing the relevant legal provisions and highlighting the changes in that regard under EU and Benelux trade mark law, this contribution will give an overview of relevant case law showing the application and evolution of the concept of bad faith under EU trade mark law.

1. EVOLUTION OF EU TRADE MARK LEGISLATION ON BAD FAITH

A. CTM AND EU TRADE MARK REGULATIONS

Ever since Council Regulation (EC) No. 40/94 of 20 December 1993 on the Community trade mark (CTM Regulation No. 40/94),[121] which established the 'Office for Harmonization in the Internal Market (trade marks and designs)' and ultimately allowed for the first CTMs to be filed in April 1996, the provisions regarding bad faith have not substantially changed. Article 51(1)(b) CTM Regulation No. 40/94 already provided the following:

Absolute grounds for invalidity

1. A Community trade mark shall be declared invalid on application to the Office or on the basis of a counterclaim in infringement proceedings,

(...)

(b) where the applicant was acting in bad faith when he filed the application for the trade mark.

---

[121] Council Regulation (EC) No 40/94 of 20 December 1993 on the Community trade mark, *OJ L* 11, 14.1.1994, p. 1–36, ELI: http://data.europa.eu/eli/reg/1994/40/oj.

Article 59(1)(b) of the European Union trade mark Regulation (EUTMR)[122] still provides for the exact same wording, simply replacing 'Community trade mark' by 'EU trade mark'.

However, as will be discussed below, important changes occurred within the framework of the EU trade mark directives harmonizing the laws of the EU Member States.

B. EU TRADE MARK DIRECTIVES

i) Changes under EU trade mark law

Going back to the First Council Directive 89/104/EEC of 21 December 1988 to approximate the laws of the Member States relating to trade marks (First Council Directive 89/104/EEC),[123] a distinction has been made between 'absolute' and 'relative' bad faith.

According to article 3(2)(d) of the First Council Directive 89/104/EEC, any Member State may provide that a trade mark shall not be registered or, if registered, shall be liable to be declared invalid where and to the extent that the application for registration of the trade mark was made in bad faith by the applicant. This provision gave the EU Member States the option to include bad faith as an absolute ground for refusal or invalidity, similar to the provisions of the CTM and EU trade mark regulations mentioned above.

Article 4(4)(g) of the First Council Directive 89/104/EEC added an optional relative ground for refusal based on bad faith when the trade mark can be confused with a mark used abroad:

> *Any Member State may furthermore provide that a trade mark shall not be registered or, if registered, shall be liable to be declared invalid where, and to the extent that:*
> *(...)*
> *(g) the trade mark is liable to be confused with a mark which was in use abroad on the filing date of the application and which is still in use there, provided that at the date of the application the applicant was acting in bad faith.*

---

[122] Regulation (EU) 2017/1001 of the European Parliament and of the Council of 14 June 2017 on the European Union trade mark, *OJ L* 154, 16.6.2017, p. 1–99, ELI: http://data.europa.eu/eli/reg/2017/1001/oj.

[123] The First Council Directive 89/104/EEC of 21 December 1988 to approximate the laws of the Member States relating to trade marks, *OJ L* 40, 11.2.1989, p. 1–7, ELI: http://data.europa.eu/eli/dir/1989/104/oj.

The European Union trade mark directive (EUTMD)[124] introduced two changes to these provisions. First, EU Members States must provide for bad faith as an absolute ground for invalidity. Bad faith as an absolute ground for refusal remains optional:

> *A trade mark shall be liable to be declared invalid where the application for registration of the trade mark was made in bad faith by the applicant. Any Member State may also provide that such a trade mark is not to be registered.*[125]

Second, the relative ground for refusal remains optional but has been limited to situations in which the mark can be confused with an earlier mark protected abroad, instead of a mark "in use abroad" as stated before:

> *Any Member State may provide that a trade mark is not to be registered or, if registered, is liable to be declared invalid where, and to the extent that the trade mark is liable to be confused with an earlier trade mark protected abroad, provided that, at the date of the application, the applicant was acting in bad faith.*[126]

ii) Impact on Benelux trade mark law

Prior to the implementation of the EUTMD, the Benelux Convention on Intellectual Property (BCIP)[127] included the following article 2.4.f regarding bad faith:

> *Does not grant the right to the mark:*
> *(…)*
> *f. the registration of a mark filed in bad faith, in particular:*
> • *1 °. the filing made with knowledge or inexcusable ignorance of the normal good faith use in the last three years in the Benelux territory of a resembling mark for similar products or services, by a third party who is not consenting to this filing;*
> • *2 °. the filing, made with knowledge, resulting from direct relations, of the normal good faith use by a third party in the last three years outside the Benelux territory, of a similar mark for similar products or services, unless this third party consented to the filing or that said knowledge has only been acquired after the applicant started using the mark in the Benelux territory."*[128] *(freely translated)*

124 Directive (EU) 2015/2436 of the European Parliament and of the Council of 16 December 2015 to approximate the laws of the Member States relating to trade marks, *OJ L* 336, 23.12.2015, p. 1–26, ELI: http://data.europa.eu/eli/dir/2015/2436/oj.

125 Article 4(2) EUTMD.

126 Article 5(4)(c) EUTMD.

127 Benelux Convention on Intellectual Property, available at https://www.boip.int/en/ip-professionals/regulations-policy/regulations#cbpi.

128 Article 2.4.f BCIP entered into force on 1 June 2018 until 1 March 2019.

The two specific situations cited in the above provision relate to 'relative' bad faith as these involve (knowledge of) earlier marks. Although these were only examples of bad faith, it was often considered that the concept of bad faith was limited to these situations, and that prior knowledge of a mark under the conditions set out in the old article 2.4.f BCIP automatically amounted to bad faith without having regard to the specific circumstances of each case.

The integration of the EUTMD into Benelux trade mark law introduced a major change by deleting this article 2.4.f BCIP. The current version of the BCIP includes a provision on bad faith as an absolute ground for invalidity in line with article 4(2) EUTMD, thereby abandoning the narrow approach to bad faith.[129]

The current BCIP does not provide for a specific relative ground for refusal or invalidity based on bad faith involving a prior mark protected abroad, as allowed pursuant to article 5(4)(c) EUTMD.

2. OVERVIEW OF EU CASE LAW ON BAD FAITH

A. GENERAL PRINCIPLE

As shown above, EU trade mark law uses an open concept of bad faith without providing for a specific definition. Nevertheless, the Court of Justice of the European Union (CJEU) ruled that bad faith is an autonomous concept of EU law, which must be given a uniform interpretation in the EU.[130] The EUIPO Trade mark Guidelines cite Advocate General Sharpston who proposed defining it as 'conduct which departs from accepted principles of ethical behaviour or honest commercial and business practices'.[131]

Advocate General Sharpston stated the above in the framework of one of the most cited cases of the CJEU regarding bad faith, namely *Lindt Goldhase*.[132] This case established the basic principle according to which all the relevant factors specific to a particular case, which pertained at the time of filing the application for registration of the sign as a CTM/EUTM, must be considered.

---

129 Article 2.2*bis*(2) BCIP entered into force on 1 March 2019.

130 Judgment of the CJEU of 27 June 2013, *Malaysia Diary*, C-320/12, EU:C:2013:435, §§29, 34–35.

131 Opinion of Advocate General Sharpston of 12 March 2009, *Lindt Goldhase*, C-529/07, EU:C:2009:148, §60.

132 Judgment of the CJEU of 11 June 2009, *Lindt Goldhase*, C-529/07, EU:C:2009:361.

Without being exhaustive, we list three different types of bad faith which have been identified in EU case law. It is only a modest attempt to categorize these cases as the open concept of bad faith allows for endless interpretations based on the specific facts of each case.

B. KNOWLEDGE OF PRIOR USE OF A SIGN BY A THIRD PARTY

In the ***Lindt Goldhase* case** mentioned above, the CJEU was asked for criteria to assess bad faith in a situation where identical or similar signs were already used, in at least one Member State, for identical or similar goods on the date of filing of the trade mark at issue. The CJEU provided a non-exhaustive list of relevant factors in this case:

- the fact that the applicant knows or must know that a third party is using, in at least one Member State, an identical or similar sign for an identical or similar product capable of being confused with the sign for which registration is sought;
- the applicant's intention to prevent that third party from continuing to use such a sign; and
- the degree of legal protection enjoyed by the third party's sign and by the sign for which registration is sought.[133]

However, the CJEU added that the knowledge of an identical or similar earlier sign for identical or similar goods or services is not sufficient in itself to support a finding of bad faith. The applicant's intention at the time when he/she files the application for registration must be considered. This is a subjective factor which must be determined by reference to the objective circumstances of the particular case.[134]

In the ***Malaysia Diary* case**, the CJEU referred to the *Lindt Goldhase* case and applied the same principles to a situation where a third party was already using a mark <u>outside of the EU</u> at the time of filing of the trade mark application at issue. The fact that the applicant knows or should know about this third party use of a mark abroad is not sufficient in itself to support a finding of bad faith.[135]

Other cases involving the knowledge of prior use of a sign developed the bad faith assessment criteria even further.

---

133 *Ibid.*, §53.

134 *Ibid.*, §§40–42.

135 Judgment of the CJEU of 27 June 2013, *Malaysia Diary*, C-320/12, EU:C:2013:435, §37.

For example, the ***Simca* case** involved the registration of the word mark SIMCA for vehicles in 2008. SIMCA was previously a famous car brand but was eventually sold to GIE PSA Peugeot Citroën, which ceased to market vehicles under this brand at the end of the 1970s. The EU General Court found that the OHIM (now EUIPO) Board of Appeal was correct to evaluate both the origin of the sign which formed the contested mark SIMCA and the earlier use of that sign in business as a mark, in particular by competing undertakings, and the commercial logic underlying the filing of the application for registration of the mark at issue, formed by that sign.[136] According to the EU General Court, 'the Board of Appeal was entitled to infer from the particular circumstances of the present case that the real purpose of the (…) application for registration of a Community trade mark was to 'free-ride' on the reputation of the [GIE PSA Peugeot Citroën]'s registered marks and to take advantage of that reputation'.[137]

More recently, the EU General Court found that the registration of a trade mark for the sign **NEYMAR** for clothing, footwear and headgear in 2013 had been made in bad faith for similar reasons, namely with the intention to 'free-ride' on the reputation of the famous football player known by the same name and to take advantage of that reputation.[138] The EU General Court took into account the fact that on the day the applicant filed the NEYMAR application, he also filed an application for registration of the word mark IKER CASILLAS, which corresponds to the name of another famous football player. This showed that the applicant possessed more than a little knowledge of the world of football.[139]

Another recent case involving prior use of a mark by a third party is especially relevant as it makes the link with the next categories of bad faith discussed under III.C and III.D, namely bad faith found independently of any intention to target a specific third party or mark. In the ***Koton* case**, the CJEU clarified the concept of bad faith as an absolute ground for invalidity.

The case concerned an application for the below figurative trade mark (the 'Stylo & Koton mark') in classes 25 ('Clothing, footwear, headgear'), 35 ('Advertising; business management; business administration; office functions') and 39 ('Transport; packaging and storage of goods; travel arrangement'):

136 Judgment of the EU General Court of 8 May 2014, *Simca*, T-327/12, EU:T:2014:240, §40.
137 *Ibid.*, §56.
138 Judgment of the EU General Court of 14 May 2019, *NEYMAR*, T-795/17, EU:T:2019:329, §51.
139 *Ibid.*, §50.

A Turkish textile company opposed this application based *i.a.* on the following trade mark, registered in classes 25 and 35:

The EUIPO upheld the opposition regarding the goods and services in classes 25 and 35 but not regarding class 39 (transportation services), because of the lack of similarity with the goods and services of the textile company's mark. The EUIPO Board of Appeal confirmed that decision, resulting in the registration of the Stylo & Koton mark for the services in class 39. The textile company did not accept the situation and filed an application for a declaration of invalidity against the Stylo & Koton mark, invoking bad faith pursuant to the former article 52(1)(b) of the Trade Mark Regulation No. 207/2009 (now article 59(1)(b) EUTMR). The textile company's application was rejected by the EUIPO Cancellation Division and Board of Appeal, and the EU General Court also dismissed the action based on the lack of similarity of the goods and services covered by the trade marks at issue.

Before the CJEU, the textile company argued that the General Court erred in law by finding that the existence of bad faith presupposes that the contested trade mark was registered for services identical with, or similar to, the goods and services in respect of which an earlier mark is registered.

The CJEU stated that bad faith applies 'where it is apparent from relevant and consistent indicia that the proprietor of an EU trade mark has filed the application for registration of that mark not with the aim of engaging fairly in competition but with the intention of undermining, in a manner inconsistent with honest practices, the interests of third parties, or with the intention of obtaining, without even targeting a specific third party, an exclusive right for purposes other than those falling within the functions of a trade mark, in particular the essential function of indicating origin'.[140]

The CJEU thus made a clear distinction between bad faith, taken up as an absolute ground for invalidity, and relative grounds for invalidity, which presuppose the existence of an earlier trade mark. According to the CJEU, in the case of an application for a declaration of invalidity based on bad faith, there is no requirement whatsoever that the applicant for that declaration is the proprietor of an earlier mark for identical or similar goods or services.[141] Again, all the circumstances relevant to the case must be taken into account, including the commercial logic behind the registration of the Stylo & Koton mark and the fact that the parties had a previous business relationship.[142]

It follows that bad faith is not always dependent on the prior knowledge of another sign. Bad faith can also be found when the applicant intends to register a mark for other illegitimate purposes.

C. NO (LEGITIMATE) INTENT TO USE THE TRADE MARK

The *Koton* case enables us to identify an important characteristic of the concept of bad faith: unlike relative grounds or other absolute grounds for refusal or invalidity, bad faith does not necessarily relate to some 'deficiency' of the trade mark at issue, such as similarity with a prior mark or the absence of distinctive character. It rather relates to the circumstances under which this trade mark has been registered.

The ***Sky* judgment** of the CJEU confirmed the above principle in a recent case which did not involve any prior third party mark. In this case, the British broadcaster and telecommunications company Sky started infringement proceedings against the company SkyKick before the UK Courts based on various EUTMs and a UK word mark including the word 'SKY', registered in

140 Judgment of the CJEU of 12 September 2019, *Koton*, C-104/18 P, EU:C:2019:724, §46.
141 *Ibid.*, §53.
142 *Ibid.*, §62.

respect of a large number of goods and services. SkyKick filed a counterclaim, essentially arguing that the Sky trade marks had been registered in bad faith because Sky did not intend to use the trade marks for all of the goods and services covered by the registrations. The referring UK court filed a request for a preliminary ruling to the CJEU, which included the following questions: can it constitute bad faith simply to apply to register a trade mark without any intention to use it in relation to the specified goods or services? If so, is it possible to conclude that the applicant made the application partly in good faith and partly in bad faith if and to the extent that the applicant had an intention to use the trade mark in relation to some of the specified goods or services, but no intention to use the trade mark in relation to other specified goods or services?

The CJEU noted that the applicant of a trade mark does not have to indicate or even to know precisely, on the date on which his or her application for registration of a mark is filed or of the examination of that application, the use the applicant will make of the mark applied for and that the applicant has a period of 5 years for commencing actual use consistent with the essential function of that trade mark.[143]

However, the CJEU referred to the Advocate General's Opinion[144] and ruled that the registration of a trade mark by an applicant without any intention to use it in relation to the goods and services covered by that registration may constitute bad faith, where there is no rationale for the application for registration in the light of the aims of EU trade mark law. The CJEU repeated its findings in *Koton* regarding the assessment to be made: bad faith may be established only if there is objective, relevant and consistent indicia tending to show that, when the application for a trade mark was filed, the trade mark applicant had the intention either of undermining, in a manner inconsistent with honest practices, the interests of third parties, or of obtaining, without even targeting a specific third party, an exclusive right for purposes other than those falling within the functions of a trade mark.[145] The CJEU also confirmed that it is possible that bad faith relates to only part of the goods or services covered by the trade mark application.[146]

We have not yet heard the last word on this specific case as appeals are still pending before the UK Courts following the *Sky* judgment of the CJEU, but it touches upon a big issue for trade mark applicants: registered trade marks

---

143 Judgment of the CJEU of 29 January 2020, *Sky*, C-371/18, EU:C:2020:45, §76.

144 Opinion of Advocate General Tanchev of 16 October 2019, *Sky*, C-371/18, EU:C:2019:864, §109.

145 Judgment of the CJEU of 29 January 2020, *Sky*, C-371/18, EU:C:2020:45, §77.

146 *Ibid.*, §81.

with overly broad descriptions of goods and services can effectively block new trade marks which could perfectly coexist if the goods and/or services of the prior mark had been specified in more detail. Nowadays, a description such as 'computer software' seems to be very vague given the number of different applications of such a concept.

In the ***Target Ventures*** **case**, the EU General Court relied on the *Koton* and *Sky* judgments of the CJEU to confirm that the concept of bad faith cannot be interpreted too restrictively. This case opposed two companies respectively called 'Target Partners GmbH' and 'Target Ventures Group Ltd'. The German company Target Partners GmbH already used its name TARGET PARTNERS as a mark and registered an EUTM for the word sign TARGET VENTURES in 2015. Target Ventures Group Ltd (the 'invalidity applicant') invoked bad faith to invalidate this EUTM. The EUIPO Cancellation Division rejected the invalidity action because it was not proven that Target Partners GmbH knew or should have known about the use of the sign TARGET VENTURES by the invalidity applicant. The EUIPO Board of Appeal confirmed this view and added that it was not proven that Target Partners GmbH's sole intention was to prevent the invalidity applicant from entering the European market. According to the Board of Appeal, Target Partners GmbH had a legitimate interest in registering the mark to expand its use of the sign TARGET VENTURES or to protect its clients from potential confusion with third parties.

The General Court annulled the Board of Appeal's decision. In the General Court's view, the Board of Appeal interpreted bad faith too restrictively because it is not necessary to target a specific third party. This means that it is also not necessary to have knowledge of such third party. For a finding of bad faith, it may indeed be sufficient to seek to obtain a trade mark without intending to use it as such.[147]

According to the General Court, Target Partners GmbH's registration of the sign TARGET VENTURES in order to prevent a likelihood of confusion with its TARGET PARTNERS mark was not in line with the functions of a trade mark, in particular the essential function of indicating origin. Indeed, it appeared that Target Partners GmbH only offered services under its TARGET PARTNERS mark.[148]

This *Target Ventures* case shows that purely defensive trade mark registrations are at risk of being declared invalid.

---

147 Decision of the EU General Court of 28 October 2020, *Target Ventures*, T-273/19, EU:T:2020:510, §§27–29.

148 *Ibid.*, §38.

Other examples of bad faith due to the absence of any (legitimate) intent to use a trade mark relate to the famous street artist **Banksy**. Over the past few years, the company Pest Control Office Limited, which is said to be linked to Banksy, has filed for various figurative EUTMs corresponding to the artist's artworks. The most probable explanation for this strategy is to obtain a legal title to invoke against any unauthorized use of Banksy's artworks while preserving the artist's anonymity. Banksy cannot invoke copyright if he/she remains anonymous. The EUIPO has already invalidated six EUTMs corresponding to Banksy artworks based on a finding of bad faith. According to the EUIPO, the EUTM applicant never had the intention to genuinely use the signs at issue as trade marks. As mentioned in one of the decisions of the EUIPO Cancellation Division, 'the contested EUTM was filed in order for Banksy to have legal rights over the sign as he could not rely on copyright rights, but that is not a function of a trade mark'.[149] Banksy opened a shop selling merchandise in an attempt to show use of the trade marks, but his/her own statements in the press convinced the EUIPO that there was no genuine intention to use the marks as trade marks to commercialise goods or provide any services in order to carve out a portion of the relevant market.

D. EVERGREENING

Evergreening refers to the practice of re-filing an application for a sign identical or highly similar to a previously registered trade mark in order to avoid a legitimate loss of rights or to otherwise take undue advantage of the trade mark system.

The EU General Court addressed the issue in its ***Pelikan* judgment**. In this case, the alleged evergreening practice consisted in the filing of a repeat application for the same mark in order to avoid the consequences entailed by total or partial revocation of earlier trade marks for reasons of non-use. The General Court confirmed that 'that fact is something which may be taken into account in order to assess whether the proprietor acted in bad faith'.[150] However, the General Court found that the trade mark applicant did not act in bad faith in the specific circumstances of the case. Indeed, the contested CTM was a (slightly) updated version of Pelikan's earlier CTMs, with some differences from these earlier marks. The General Court considered that the evolution over time of a logo

---

149 Decision of the EUIPO Cancellation Division of 18 May 2021, Cancellation No 39 873 C, available at https://euipo.europa.eu/eSearch/#details/trademarks/017981629.

150 Decision of the EU General Court of 13 December 2012, *Pelikan*, T-136/11, EU:T:2012:689, §27.

intended as the graphic representation of a mark constitutes normal business practice.[151]

The ***Luceo* case** concerned a practice in which an applicant made a successive chain of applications for registration of national trade marks for the same sign every six months, which corresponds to the period allowed to claim priority according to the former article 29(1) of the Trade Mark Regulation No. 207/2009 (now article 34(1) EUTMR). Those national applications were successively cancelled due to non-payment of the registration fee, but as soon as a third party applied for an EUTM covering an identical or similar sign, it allowed the applicant to apply for an EUTM claiming priority for it by relying on the last link of the chain of applications for registration of national trade marks. The artificial priority allowed the applicant to oppose the third party application and use its blocking position to negotiate a financial arrangement with this third party. This applicant was obviously found to be in bad faith, as it could not prove any legitimate intention to use the mark at issue other than to block the third party and derive an economic advantage from it.[152]

More recently, the EU General Court had to assess bad faith in the context of a classic evergreening practice, namely the practice of re-filing an EUTM application covering a sign identical to one or more earlier EUTMs with the (often undeclared) purpose of avoiding the obligation to prove genuine use. It follows from article 18(1) EUTMR that an EUTM must be put to genuine use within a period of five years following its registration. Conversely, this rule enables the owner of an EUTM to enforce its rights, for example in opposition proceedings, without having to prove genuine use of the EUTM during the first five years after its registration.[153] As proof of use can be a burdensome exercise, EUTM owners can be tempted to file a new EUTM every five years to avoid this obligation.

The ***Monopoly* case** related to the re-filing of the MONOPOLY word mark by Hasbro. The EU General Court referred to its *Pelikan* judgment and stated that 'although repeat filings of a mark are not prohibited, the fact remains that such a filing which is carried out in order to avoid the consequences entailed by non-use of earlier marks may constitute a relevant factor which is capable of establishing bad faith on the part of the person who filed that mark'.[154] The EU General Court took into account several factors in order to confirm the EUIPO Board of Appeal's finding of bad faith, including the following:

151 *Ibid.*, §36.
152 Decision of the EU General Court of 7 July 2016, *Luceo*, T-82/14, EU:T:2016:396, §§144–145.
153 See also article 47(2) EUTMR.
154 Decision of the EU General Court of 21 April 2021, *Monopoly*, T-663/19, EU:T:2021:211, §57.

- Hasbro, the EUTM applicant, had relied on the contested mark and on the earlier marks in the context of two sets of opposition proceedings. It stated, in that regard, that the decisions by which the applicant had been successful in those proceedings were based on the contested mark, as, for that mark, it was not necessary to provide proof of genuine use. The EUTM applicant thus actually derived an advantage from its repeat filing strategy;
- it was apparent from the testimony of one of the employees of Hasbro, given at an oral hearing held during the proceedings before the EUIPO Board of Appeal, that being able to rely on the registration of one mark without the need to prove use was a benefit to the applicant and that it was something that was considered by all brand owners;
- according to the witness statement, it was an accepted industry practice at the relevant time for companies to file applications for registration of trade marks that were already the subject of existing EU registrations and to include in those new applications goods or services that were covered by the earlier marks. In the EUIPO Board of Appeal's view, this clearly implied that using such a strategy was intentional.[155]

The testimony of one of Hasbro's employees seems to have been instrumental in enabling the finding of bad faith to be reached in this particular case, but EUTM owners will nevertheless need to provide a reasonable explanation when making repeat filings in the future.

3. CONCLUSION

While the legal provisions regarding bad faith have not changed in EU trade mark regulations since the creation of the first CTMs in 1996, the harmonisation of the concept of bad faith in the EU Member States has evolved through EU trade mark directives and especially the EUTMD.

Bad faith is an autonomous concept of EU law but has not been uniformly defined, and probably never will be given its subjective nature and its various possible applications. The extensive case law of the CJEU and the EU General Court has enabled the concept to be clarified and has provided for at least some legal certainty, but future case law will most certainly be useful in view of the evolving interpretations of bad faith under EU trade mark law.

155 *Ibid.*, §§58–64 and §§70–72.

VII. BE CAREFUL WHEN ACQUIRING TRADE MARKS WITH AN INDICATION OF TRADITION SUCH AS "SINCE 1875"! (ART 58(1) (C) EUTMR – MISLEADING USE)

Alexander SCHNIDER

Many businesses register their company name together with the time of establishment as trade marks, such as EUTM 000183384, "Fruit of the Loom the Original since 1851", EUTM 000490029, "NUS since 1933", EUTM 000404418, "ANCHOR STEAM BEER Made in San Francisco since 1896" and many more. The reason for doing so is obvious: adding such an element to a trade mark indicates a relevant tradition, a relevant longevity of business, indicative of brand continuity.

Whilst acquiring the corresponding trade mark proprietor entirely via a share deal should pose no issues with regard to the question whether or not such "indication of tradition" may become misleading because the trade mark proprietor remains the same, care must be taken when acquiring such trade marks by way of an asset deal. In the first decision ever dealing with such a "tradition"-trade mark in the context of an asset deal, the Austrian Supreme Court provides some guidelines with regard to the question when and why a trade mark may be revoked due to actual misleading use under Art 58 para 1(c) EUTMR and corresponding national provisions, such as section 33c of the Austrian Trademark Act.

1. TRADE MARK REVOCATION EU CASE LAW UNDER ART. 12 PARA. 2 LIT B) OF THE TRADE MARK DIRECTIVE 89/104/EEC

Until recently, the ground for forfeiture of an EU trade mark under Art. 58 para. 1.it. c) EUTMR was rather uncharted territory. So far, and on EU-level, the

European Court of Justice ("ECJ") has only dealt once with the prior identical provision concerning the revocation of a trade mark as laid down in Art. 12 para. 2 lit b) of the Trademark Directive 89/104/EEC in the decision C-259/04, Elizabeth Emanuel. This decision concerned a name trade mark, that is to say the name of a fashion designer, acquired by a company together with the entire business operations for the production of the branded designer goods and the associated goodwill. Based on the following principles, the ECJ held that the new trade mark owner's use of the "Elizabeth Emanual" trade mark for designating fashion products is not misleading in light of the transfer of the designer's entire business operations together with the trade mark.

Under Art. 12 para. 2 lit b) of the Trademark Directive 89/104/EEC, the revocation of a trade mark requires actual or potential misleading of the public, which must relate to the characteristics and properties of the marked product (ECJ, C-259/04, paras 47 and 48 in conjunction with para 53). In the case of the name mark "Elizabeth Emanuel" in question, the misconception of the public that the designer was involved in the creation is not sufficient for the product continuity, in particular the expected quality of the designer's goods, to be misleading, especially if the business and the goodwill were transferred with the mark (ECJ, C-259/04, paras. 44, 48 and 51 in connection with para. 53). The trade mark must in itself be capable of deceiving the public as to the nature, quality or geographical origin of the marked products (para. 49).

2. NEW CASE LAW BY THE AUSTRIAN SUPREME COURT UNDER ART. 58 PARA. 1(C) EUTMR WITH REGARD TO ASSET DEALS

In March 2021, the Elizabeth Emanuel decision mentioned received its first update by the Austrian Supreme Court. In its decision 4 Ob 221/20h – Pauscha (Vienna Appellate Court's docket number 1 R 82/20, Vienna Commercial Court's docket number 68 Cg 33/19p), the Austrian Supreme Court dealt with the following facts giving rise to the revocation of the following word-device EUTM due to actual misleading use:

The application for:

Pauscha
Austria
·since 1875·

EUTM 012315719, was filed on 15 November 2013, and the trade mark was registered on 19 March 2014. The trade mark was registered for the following goods and services in the following classes:

Class 20: goods of wood, barrels, drums not of metal, barrels [small] not of metal, in particular small barrels, storage barrels and cooking stands in round and oval form;

Class 37 building, repairing, maintenance, repairs and restoration, in particular of wooden barrels and wine barrels; and

Class 40 material processing, in particular wood working for the manufacture of wooden barrels.

The Plaintiff and the Defendant are both barrel-makers based in Carinthia, Austria, and the revocation action based on misleading use was filed with the Vienna Commercial Court in response to an infringement claim pursued by the Defendant based on the now revoked trade mark. The Defendant acquired the word-device mark in question and used the EU trade mark to identify its barrel maker business as well as its wooden barrels. The trade mark in question had the following history until the Defendant acquired it:

In 1875, a person having the family name "Pauscha" founded a barrel maker business under this very name in a territory that is now Slovenia. In 1951, the Pauscha family relocated the Pauscha barrel maker business to Wolfsberg, Austria. In 1998, the Pauscha family incorporated their company into a newly founded limited liability company, which subsequently became subject to bankruptcy proceedings in 2010. After the Pauscha family acquired the company from the insolvency proceedings, they founded a new limited liability company under the name Pauscha Fassbinderei.

In May 2011, one of the Pauscha family members, Mr. Klaus Pauscha, left Pauscha Fassbinderei and founded his own limited liability company, Klaus Pauscha & Partner. From this point on, the Pauscha Fassbinderei limited liability company was continued without the operational involvement of the Pauscha family alongside Klaus Pauscha & Partner, its direct competitor. In November 2013 Pauscha Fassbinderei applied for the EUTM in question, which was registered shortly before Pauscha Fassbinderei became insolvent and was thus finally wound down so that it ceased to exist.

The EUTM in question, the Internet domain www.pauscha.at and the machines of the Pauscha Fassbinderei limited liability company were initially acquired by an asset purchaser, and in April 2014 that asset purchaser subsequently sold all of these assets (EUTM, Internet domain and machines) to an Italian purchaser. In April 2014, the aforementioned Italian purchaser founded the Defendant, which set up a new production site in Wolfsberg, Austria, and the 'PAUSCHA Austria – since 1875' EUTM was transferred to the Defendant. Apart from the EUTM, the domain and the machines, three employees of the former Pauscha Fassbinderei limited liability company were also taken over. From this moment on, two barrel-makers using the name Pauscha were active in Wolfsberg, Austria – the Defendant, operating under the EUTM and the Internet domain as well as the Plaintiff, a member of the Pauscha family, operating under the Pauscha family name.

The Defendant manufactures its wooden barrels according to the tradition of an Italian family whose barrel maker tradition reaches back more than 240 years. However, their wooden barrels differ from the Pauscha wooden barrels in the way they are made, in their appearance, and the stave thickness; the Defendant's barrels are thicker. The type and tradition of the production of wine barrels are of great relevance for the buyers of the barrels, particularly for winegrowers, because the construction affects the taste of the wine stored in them. On the Defendant's website, hosted at www.pauscha.at, the Defendant stated, among other things, as follows: "*Our traditional craft business, Pauscha Austria, has been producing barriques and casks for the refinement of wines and distillates since 1875. The company Pauscha Austria – since 1875 continues the long tradition of barrel making.*"

3. FACTUAL DIFFERENCES BETWEEN ELIZABETH EMANUAL AND PAUSCHA

From the above facts, the factual differences between the Austrian Pauscha case and the ECJ's Elizabeth Emanuel case are obvious.

Firstly, whilst in the Elizabeth Emanual case, the entire business operations were transferred to the purchaser, only some assets (the Internet domain Pauscha.at, several machines and three employees) were transferred to the purchaser in the Austrian Pauscha case. Therefore, the EUTM purchaser in the Elizabeth Emanuel case profited from business continuity, whilst the EUTM purchaser in the Pauscha case did not.

Secondly, whilst the EUTM only comprised a name in the ECJ's Elizabeth Emanuel case, in the Austrian Pauscha case the EUTM did not only comprise a family and company name, namely "Pauscha", but also a time-element, namely "since 1875", which indicates when the original trade mark owner commenced his business.

4. THE AUSTRIAN COURTS' DECISIONS

In the first instance, the Vienna Commercial Court dismissed the main claim for a declaration of invalidity of the EU trade mark and granted the contingent claim for revoking the trade mark with effect from 7 April 2014. It also granted a claim for injunctive relief based on the Austrian Unfair Competition Act, a claim to remove all misleading communications and publication of the judgment. The Vienna Commercial Court mainly held that the labelling of the Defendant's wooden barrels gives winegrowers the impression that the Defendant, by using the EUTM "PAUSCHA Austria – since 1875", continued without interruption the original business and the tradition of craftsmanship of the Pauscha family. Therefore, the Vienna Commercial Court noted a likelihood of misleading consumers within the meaning of Article 58 para. 1 lit c) of the EUTMR because the Defendant produced barrels at a new production site according to its own (Italian styled) design without being able to fall back on the know-how of the Pauscha family's business.

The Vienna Court of Appeal upheld this decision and affirmed the ground for revocation under Article 58 para 1 lit. c) EUTMR because the Defendant was neither the universal successor to the Pauscha family business nor had it taken over the production method and processing the wooden barrels from this family business. Because of the reference in the EUTM "PAUSCHA Austria – since 1875" to the 145 years' of the Pauscha family's experience, the Vienna Court of Appeal held that the public associated this EUTM with the special quality of a product manufactured in a traditional Austrian manner.

The Austrian Supreme Court upheld this result. In doing so, the Austrian Supreme Court also provided some important guidelines for acquiring and using a EUTM that contains a time designation, such as "since 1875".

Under Art. 58 para. 1 lit c) EUTMR, the misleading character must relate (in particular) to the nature, quality or geographical origin of the marked goods or services. The additional element "as a result of the use made of it" clarifies that the misleading character may be due solely to the actual use made of the EU trade mark. Thus, for revocation purposes, the EU trade mark must have the potential to mislead the public by its actual use alone. In other words: the likelihood of misleading the public must therefore result solely from the use of the trade mark and thus from the sign itself. Indications outside the sign (e.g.

in advertising) or specific types of use (e.g. omissions or explanatory additions) must therefore be disregarded (to that effect, see also the German literature in this regard, such as *Thiering* in *Ströbele/Hacker/Thiering*, MarkenG[12] §49 mn 49; *Inger/Rohnke*, MarkenG[3] §49 mn 41; *Fezer*, Markenrecht[4] §49 mn 35; for the Austrian literature, see, e.g., *Schwarzenbacher* in *Kucsko/Schumacher*, marken. schutz[3] §33c mn 1;).

As explained above and as already expressed by the ECJ in the Elizabeth Emanuel case, the misleading character must relate to the characteristics and properties of the marked product concerning its type, nature, quality or geographical origin. Accordingly, the Austrian Supreme Court held that misconceptions that the public had about the continuity of the undertaking or – generally speaking – undertaking-related deceptions cannot, in principle, in themselves lead to the revocation of a trade mark, except in the case of bad faith (cf. ECJ C-259/04 – Elizabeth Emanuel, para 50). According to the Austrian Supreme Court, however, this is not the case if the public associates the company assumed to be behind the trade mark (or, above all, in the case of a name trade mark, the person) with a particular quality and grade which the goods or services no longer have (to that extent, see also, e.g., the German literature as per *Thiering* in *Ströbele/Hacker/Thiering*, MarkenG[12] §49 para 51).

In the Austrian case we are concerned with, the Austrian Supreme Court further held that the EU trade mark not only contained a time designation but that "since 1875" is also to be qualified as an indication of tradition and that, if such an indication of tradition subsequently leads to misconceptions on the part of the public as to the quality characteristics of the marked product, then, according to the principles set out above, this misleading character is also caused solely by the use of the trade mark as such (cf. on the similar case of a subsequent transfer, German Federal Supreme Court, I ZR 19/78; EUIPO R0697/2008-1; cf. also *Salomonowitz* in *Kucsko/Schumacher*, marken.schutz[3] §11 mn 32). The view expressed by *Thiering* (in *Ströbele/Hacker/Thiering*, MarkenG[12] §49 mn 56), according to which Art. 58 para. 1) lit. c) EUTMR only depends on a change in the meaning of the trade mark itself and that a misleading character due to other circumstances (such as a transfer of the seat or a trade mark) is not to be subsumed under this, thus proved to be too narrow for the Austrian Supreme Court.

When assessing whether the use of the "PAUSCHA Austria – since 1875" EUTM by the Defendant, which was founded in 2014 by its owners, who have a barrel maker tradition reaching back more than 240 years, was misleading, the Austrian Supreme Court firstly concluded that the EUTM in question combined the family name "Pauscha" with the indication of tradition "since

1875" and thus referred to the approximately 150-year family tradition of the Pauscha family in the production of the designated wooden barrels, but not to the more than 240-year tradition of the Defendant's owner family. Secondly, the Austrian Supreme Court held that the public associates such a long tradition in barrel making, even if they are winegrowers and thus no ordinary consumers, with particular perceptions of the quality and grade of the designated products, which are based on the fact that a considerable amount of experience can be drawn on in production and that the production process or the quality characteristics determining it have proven themselves over many decades. In this sense, it was also recognised in other case law that the public associates special experience and ideas of quality regarding a long-standing tradition (cf. Austrian Supreme Court's Guiding Principles summarised in RS0078638).

In other words: the indication of tradition "since 1875" in the "PAUSCHA Austria – since 1875" EUTM in question did, in the perception of the relevant target audience of winegrowers, not only refer to the continuity of the original Pauscha family company, which ceased to exist due to having been wound down in the course of its insolvency proceedings, but above all to the tradition of production and craftsmanship of the Pauscha family in the production of the "Pauscha barrels" and thus the specific quality characteristics of this product, such as correspondingly branded wine barrels.

As, according to the public's (in particular the winegrowers') perception, the production method and the stave thickness of the Pauscha barrels are decisive for the compliance with these quality characteristics, especially since the construction is decisive for the taste of the wine and the Defendant does not produce Pauscha wooden barrels, but barrels according to the tradition of its Italian owner family, whereas the Defendant uses a different production method and thicker types of wood and these differences affect the taste of the wine and give it a flavour which the public does not associate with the use of Pauscha wooden barrels, the Austrian Supreme Court summarised that the misleading nature of the use of the "PAUSCHA Austria – since 1875" EUTM in question not only related to the inaccurate perception of a business continuity in terms of the original Pauscha family company, but more importantly also with regard to the nature and quality of the marked products within the meaning of Art. 58 para. 1 lit. c) EUTMR.

The EUTM was revoked entirely with effect from 7 April 2014 for the following reasons: firstly, the former trade mark owner, i.e. Pauscha Fassbinderei limited liability company, legitimately used the EUTM in question by not only continuing the business of the original Pauscha family business, but also by producing barrels in the corresponding Pauscha tradition. Secondly, however, the EUTM was subsequently transferred to the Defendant in 2014, who from that time on did not fulfil those two requirements.

The entire revocation might seem surprising given that the Austrian courts only established that the EUTM in question was solely used for wine barrels and as a company designation. In contrast, the trade mark registration also covered other products and services (see above classification for details). In this context, the Austrian Supreme Court countered the Defendant's corresponding argument seeking only a partial cancellation by stating that the misleading character according to Article 58 para. 2 EUTMR would also apply to all other product categories. In addition, the goods and services in class 20 refer to wooden barrels and barrels and cooking stands can also be assigned to this class of goods whilst classes 37 and 40 refer to services relating to the manufacture or repair of wooden barrels, which is why the use of the EUTM for wooden barrels also covers these services. From this, it can be concluded that at least the Austrian courts would apply Article 58 para. 1 lit c) EUTMR in so far more generously as that is fulfilling this revocation ground only for some specific goods and/or services will also have an impact on similar registered goods and services which (also) are aimed at such goods for which the actual misleading EUTM use was established. Therefore, it is to be expected that the Austrian courts will in all likelihood not evoke the revocation ground laid down in article 58 para.1 lit c) EUTMTR, overly formalistic in this respect, in the future. This also means that defendants should not expect their EUTMs to remain at least partially safe from revocation in cases where they misleadingly used their EUTM only for one product or service.

5. LESSONS LEARNED CONCERNING EUTMS CONTAINING A (COMPANY) NAME AND A TIME INDICATION

Bearing in mind that trade marks can be transferred via an asset deal and that trade marks can continue to exist even in the event of the insolvency of the trade mark proprietor under Article 20 EUTMR, the first lesson learned from the Austrian Supreme Court's decision and the history of the "PAUSCHA Austria – since 1875" EUTM is that anyone who solely acquires a EUTM comprising a time and/or tradition indication (but not the entire business associated with that EUTM) must check whether they can live up to the expectations associated with the corresponding indication, particularly in cases where the time indication also suggests a certain production method or production tradition.

In this respect, it is worthwhile noting that, at least in light of the present Austrian Supreme Court decision, it seems irrelevant whether production methods generally are subject to change from time to time when the tradition and corresponding long-standing experience is incorporated into such EUTM, respectively the EUTM's time indication. In other words: even though the original Pauscha production method will have changed since its origin in 1875, the further development of that production method would also be part of that production tradition.

Second, in the case where the EUTM acquirer did not acquire the entire business operations together with the EUTM and the EUTM acquirer cannot live up to any expectations arising out of a EUTM's time and or tradition indication, it seems worthwhile to use the EUTM without that indication. In many cases, just as in the present case, time and/or tradition indications specified in years such as "since 1875" do not add anything to the EUTM's distinctiveness so that it may also be genuinely used without it, e.g. "PAUSCHA Austria" without "since 1875". Otherwise, any potential misleading use comprising the time and/ or tradition indication incorporated in the EUTM may lead to the revocation of the entire EUTM. If a genuine use without the time and/or tradition indication is not possible, it seems worthwhile to avoid any misleading effect by adding statements, claims or other information that may remedy any inaccurate impression. However, the EUTM proprietor will have to consider the target audiences and their possible perception of the EUTM.

In any case, EUTMs containing time indications should be scrutinised in the course of asset transactions, and the above case law should be considered, particularly in the course of corresponding trade mark due diligence.

VIII. APPROPRIATE JURISDICTION OF EUTM DISPUTES IN AN ONLINE WORLD

Gerard KELLY and Jane BOURKE

Since the EU trade mark was introduced 25 years ago, there has been a monumental transformation in the way business is carried out in the EU particularly with the advent of online activity. As the ecommerce market has evolved and global online sales have grown, the national courts of EU Member States and the Court of Justice of the European Union (CJEU) have had to tackle the issue of online targeting when determining the correct forum for EUTM infringement proceedings. This chapter examines the legislation on EU jurisdiction in respect of European trade marks (EUTMs) and how the case law of the CJEU dealing with jurisdiction concerning EUTMs has developed.

As the two relevant EU regulations affecting EUTM jurisdiction – Brussels Regulation (EC) No 44/2001[156] (Brussels I) and the 2017 EU Trade Mark Regulation[157] (the EUTMR) (discussed below) – have been amended, below we provide a brief history of these revisions to act as an aide memoire before launching into a summary of the more pertinent cases.

1. JURISDICTION IN CROSS BORDER EU DISPUTES – BRUSSELS I RECAST

On 22 December 2000, Brussels I was adopted, replacing the 1968 Brussels Convention.[158] The Brussels Recast Regulation[159] (Brussels I Recast) came into effect from 10 January 2015, replacing Brussels I.

156 Council Regulation (EC) No 44/2001 of 22 December 2000 on jurisdiction and the recognition and enforcement of judgments in civil and commercial matters.

157 Regulation (EU) 2017/1001 of the European Parliament and of the Council of 14 June 2017 on the European Union trade mark.

158 The Brussels Convention on jurisdiction and the enforcement of judgments in civil and commercial matters, subsequently amended by conventions on the accession to that Convention of new Member States.

159 Regulation (EU) No 1215/2012 of the European Parliament and of the Council of 12 December 2012 on jurisdiction and the recognition and enforcement of judgments in civil and commercial matters.

Brussels I Recast determines where legal proceedings can take place and the enforcement of judgments in the EU Member States. The scope of Brussels I Recast is that it should cover all the main civil and commercial matters apart from certain well-defined matters. The rules of jurisdiction should be highly predictable and founded on the principle that jurisdiction is usually based on the defendant's domicile. It follows that the general rule is that, regardless of their nationality, a defendant domiciled in a Member State shall be sued in the courts of that Member State.[160] In addition, there should be alternative grounds of jurisdiction based on a close connection between the court and the action or in order to facilitate the sound administration of justice. Article 24(4) of Brussels I Recast confers exclusive jurisdiction on national courts in proceedings concerning specific matters including the registration or validity of trade marks.

Notably following Brexit, from 1 January 2021, the UK was no longer subject to the Brussels I Recast. At the time of writing the UK had applied to join the Lugano Convention 2007[161]; however on 4 May 2021 the EU Commission formally communicated to the European Parliament and the Council of the European Union its opposition to this application.

2. EXCLUSIVE JURISDICTION IN TRADE MARK DISPUTES

The EUTRM[162] has exclusive jurisdiction[163] to deal with certain actions in respect of EUTMs. The EUTMR came into effect on 1 October 2017, repealing and replacing Regulation (EC) No. 207/2009 (the 2009 Regulation).[164] Prior to the 2009 Regulation, Council Regulation (EC) No 40/94[165] governed jurisdiction in respect of Community trade marks (CTMs) (as they were then).

In his opinion in *Coty Germany GmbH v First Note Perfumes NV*[166] Advocate General Jääskinen noted that the 2009 Regulation had a character of *lex specialis* in relation to the rules provided for by Brussels I. As such,

160 Article 4 Brussels Recast Regulation.

161 The Lugano Convention on jurisdiction and the recognition and enforcement of judgments in civil and commercial matters determines jurisdiction between the EU and certain members of the European Free Trade Association.

162 Regulation (EU) 2017/1001 of the European Parliament and of the Council of 14 June 2017 on the European Union trade mark.

163 Article 124 EUTMR.

164 Council Regulation (EC) No 207/2009 of 26 February 2009 on the Community trade mark.

165 Council Regulation (EC) No 40/94 of 20 December 1993 on the Community trade mark.

166 Case C-360/12.

Article 122(2) EUTMR excludes the general provisions in Brussels I Recast set out in Articles 4, 6, 7 and 35 in respect of disputes concerning the infringement and validity of EUTMs.

Chapter 6 (Articles 122 to 135) of the EUTMR governs jurisdiction and procedure in legal actions relating to trade marks. Article 124 of the EUTMR deals specifically with jurisdiction over infringement and validity; it provides that the EUTM courts shall have exclusive jurisdiction in relation to the following matters:

1. infringement actions (permitted under national law) and actions in respect of threatened infringement relating to EUTMs;
2. actions for declarations of non-infringement (permitted under national law);
3. actions brought as a result of acts referred to in Article 11(2); and
4. counterclaims for revocation or for declaration of invalidity of the EUTM pursuant to Article 128.

Article 125 of the EUTMR governs international jurisdiction; it provides the following:

1. Subject to the provisions of the EUTMR and Article 122 of Brussels I Recast, proceedings in respect of the actions and claims referred to in Article 124 shall be brought in the courts of the EU Member State in which the defendant is domiciled or, if he is not domiciled in any of the EU Member States, in which he has an establishment;
2. If the defendant is neither domiciled nor has an establishment in any of the EU Member States, such proceedings shall be brought in the courts of the EU Member State in which the plaintiff is domiciled or, if he is not domiciled in any of the EU Member States, in which he has an establishment;
3. If neither the defendant nor the plaintiff is so domiciled or has such an establishment, such proceedings shall be brought in the courts of the EU Member State where the Office has its seat;
4. Notwithstanding 1,2 and 3 above
   (a) Article 25 of Brussels I Recast shall apply if the parties agree that a different EU trade mark court shall have jurisdiction;
   (b) Article 26 of Brussels I Recast shall apply if the defendant enters an appearance before a different EU trade mark court; and
5. Proceedings in respect of the actions and claims referred to in Article 124 of the EUTMR, with the exception of actions for a declaration of non-infringement of an EU trade mark, may also

be brought in the courts of the EU Member State in which the act of infringement has been committed or threatened, or in which an act referred to in Article 11(2) has been committed.

3. LOCATION LOCATION LOCATION

Historically, the provisions that have given rise to difficulty are Articles 125(1) and 125(5) of the EUTMR (Article 97(1) and Article 97(5) of the 2009 regulation). In particular, the national courts of EU Member States have grappled with the concept of 'the Member State in which the act of infringement has been committed or threatened' set out in Article 125(5) of the EUTMR.

Article 125(1) of the EUTMR provides that claims referred to in Article 124 shall be brought in the courts of the EU Member State in which the defendant is domiciled or, if he is not domiciled in any of the EU Member States, in which he has an establishment. Article 125(5) of that Regulation states that the applicant may 'also' bring its action before the courts of the EU Member State 'in which the act of infringement has been committed or threatened.'

Articles 126(1) and 126(2) of the EUTMR distinguish the territorial scope of the national courts of EU Member States under Articles 125(1) and 125(5). Where an action is brought under Article 126(1) based on Article 125(1) to (4), the court has jurisdiction in respect of acts of infringement committed or threatened within the territory of any of the EU Member States. Where an action is brought before such a court under Article 126(5) based on Article 125(5), the court has jurisdiction only in respect of acts committed or threatened within the territory of the EU Member State in which that court is situated.

4. L'ORÉAL SA AND OTHERS V EBAY INTERNATIONAL AG AND OTHERS[167]

Significant developments in this area started about 10 years ago, where in *L'Oréal SA,* although not a jurisdictional case, the CJEU's consideration of online targeting has had an impact on case law in this area and deserves a brief mention. L'Oréal issued trade mark infringement proceedings in the UK against eBay for infringing its CTMs by selling counterfeit L'Oréal products. The CJEU held that the website 'www.ebay.co.uk' appeared to be targeting consumers in

---

167 C-324/09.

the territory covered by the CTM, therefore the offers for sale on that website fall within the scope of the EU rules on intellectual property.

A question on the territorial scope of EU law where non-EEA goods are sold in the EEA was referred to the CJEU. The Court held that triggering Article 5 of Directive 89/104 and Article 9 of Regulation No 40/94 is sufficient to show that goods, not previously marketed in the EU but bearing a CTM, are offered for sale online if advertisements are targeting EU consumers.

There is a school of thought that questions the applicability of the *L'Oréal SA* decision as it ensured the application of European trade mark law in trade mark infringement cases involving online targeting (outside the EEA) to consumers in the EU territory not the issue of jurisdiction within the EEA. However, as seen in later cases, this decision proves significant and continues to be applied by the CJEU.

5. WINTERSTEIGER AG V PRODUCTS 4U SONDERMASCHINENBAU GMBH[168]

The first trade mark case to focus on online activities was in 2012 in *Wintersteiger AG v Products 4U Sondermaschinenbau GmbH* which involved a reference from Austria's Supreme Court concerning the determination of international courts in relation to a national trade mark (not an EUTM). Nonetheless it is an important case in the development of jurisdiction in circumstances where infringement occurs online. Wintersteiger – an Austrian manufacturer of ski and snowboard tools – owned the Austrian trade mark 'Wintersteiger'. Products 4U is an undertaking established in Germany that also develops and sells ski and snowboard tools. Crucially there was no relationship between the parties. In 2008 Products 4U registered the word 'Wintersteiger' through the search service provided by Google AdWords. Wintersteiger issued injunctive proceedings in the Austrian courts claiming that, by placing the advertisement on 'google.de', Products 4U infringed its Austrian trade mark. Products 4U disputed the international jurisdiction of the Austrian courts on the basis that the advertisement was only intended for German customers. Although the service was restricted to searches carried out through the top-level domain site.de, the Internet site was still accessible in Austria.

In essence, the referring Court asked the CJEU to confirm what criteria are to be used in determining jurisdiction under Article 5(3) of Brussels I in circumstances

168 C-523/10.

where the alleged infringing act is different from the place where the trade mark is registered. The Court explained that the expression *"place where the harmful event occurred or may occur"* in Article 5(3) of Regulation No 44/2001 is intended to cover both the place where the damage occurred and the place of the event giving rise to it. Referring to Joined Cases C-509/09 and C-161/10 *eDate Advertising and Others [2011] ECR I-10269*, the Court noted that the purpose of the expression 'the place or places where the damage occurred or may have occurred' set out in Article 5(3) is to allow the rights holder to opt to sue in either of two places on the basis that both could be important for the claimant in terms of evidence and conduct of proceedings. Having regard to Joined Cases C-236/08 to C-238/08 *Google France and Google* [2010] ECR I-2417, and *L'Oréal and Others*, the Court noted that the courts in the EU Member State are best placed to assess whether the activity infringes the trade mark in question. It also confirmed that Brussels I Recast must be interpreted with reference to the scheme and purpose of that regulation which included the foreseeability of jurisdiction, thus enabling the applicant to easily identify the jurisdiction in which he may sue and for the defendant to reasonably foresee before which court he may be sued. As a result, the CJEU concluded that Article 5(3) of Regulation No 44/2001 must be interpreted as providing that a claimant may bring an infringement action in either the courts of the EU Member State in which the trade mark is registered or the courts of the EU Member State where the advertiser is established.

Wintersteiger provides clarity on the meaning of Article 5(3) of Regulation No 44/2001 by confirming the application of its rules when the event giving rise to the alleged damage occurred via the internet.

6. COTY GERMANY GMBH V FIRST NOTE PERFUMES NV[169]

In 2014 *Coty Germany GmbH v First Note Perfumes NV* was decided. In that case the claimant brought an action in Germany claiming the distribution of the defendant's perfume infringed Coty's three-dimensional CTM for a perfume bottle. The proceedings also involved claims for unlawful comparative advertising and unfair imitation. First Note, a perfume wholesaler established in Belgium, sold the perfume to Stefan P who took delivery of the products in Belgium and subsequently resold the perfumes in Germany. On appeal the action was dismissed. The Appellate Court agreed with the Court of First Instance that the German courts had no international jurisdiction to deal with this matter. Coty appealed this decision to the Bundesgerichtshof (The Federal

169 C-360/12.

Court of Germany) on a point of law relying on infringement of its CTM and unfair competition practices.

The Bundesgerichtshof referred the following questions to the CJEU:

> 1. Is Article 93(5) of Regulation … No 40/94 to be interpreted as meaning that an act of infringement is committed in one Member State (Member State A), within the meaning of [that provision], in the case where, as a result of an act in another Member State (Member State B), there is participation in the infringement in the first-named Member State (Member State A)?
> 2. Is Article 5(3) of Regulation … No 44/2001 to be interpreted as meaning that the harmful event occurred in one Member State (Member State A) if the tortious act which is the subject of the action or from which claims are derived was committed in another Member State (Member State B) and consists in participation in the tortious act (principal act) which took place in the first-named Member State (Member State A)?

In response to the first question the CJEU noted that the concept of 'the Member State in which the act of infringement has been committed or threatened', referred to in Article 93(5), must be interpreted independently of the concept of 'the place where the harmful event occurred or may occur' referred to in Article 5(3) Brussels I. As a result, the duality of linking factors (the place of the event giving rise to the damage and that where the damage occurred) accepted by the CJEU in previous cases cannot automatically be applied to Article 93(5) of Regulation No 40/94. The CJEU considered that context and purpose needed to be factored into an interpretation of Article 93(5) of Regulation No 40/94. The Court further noted that there would be a conflict of provisions between Articles 93(5) and Articles 94(2) of that Regulation if jurisdiction was based on the place where the alleged infringement produces its effects, on the basis that the wording of Article 94(2) limits the jurisdiction of CTM courts under Article 93(5) to acts committed or threatened in the EU Member State where the court seized is situated. The CJEU was influenced by the written opinion of Advocate General Jääskinen who noted that the linking factor relates to active conduct on the part of the person causing that infringement. Therefore, the CJEU concluded that Article 93(5) does not allow jurisdiction to be established to hear an infringement action against the original seller who did not himself act in the EU Member State where the court seized is situated.

In relation to the second question, the CJEU noted that jurisdiction regarding the unfair competition element of the action needed to be determined under Article 5(3) of Brussels I. The CJEU examined the 'place where the harmful event occurred or may occur' in Article 5(3). In conclusion the CJEU confirmed that the causal event occurred and the named defendant acted in Belgium, outside the jurisdiction of the court where it was seized.

The issues raised in *Coty* were novel in that the CJEU had to apply the rules of jurisdiction regarding a defendant whose alleged actions contributed to the infringing acts by a third party in another EU Member State as if the defendant had acted in the jurisdiction of the court seized. The Coty judgment confirms that the linking factor pursuant to Article 93(5) of Regulation No 40/94 refers to the EU Member State where the act giving rise to the alleged infringement occurred or may occur.

7. AMS NEVE LTD AND OTHERS V HERITAGE AUDIO SL AND PEDRO RODRÍGUEZ ARRIBAS[170]

More recently in 2019 the CJEU considered the application of Article 97(5) of the 2009 Regulation in *AMS Neve*. The applicant, claiming infringement of its EUTM and national trade marks, brought proceedings in the UK's Intellectual Property and Enterprise Court (IPEC). Evidence submitted by the applicants' contained screenshots from the defendant's website, highlighting the fact that offers for sale were made in English, and that the UK was listed as a distributor. The defendant company was established in Spain, and the sole director of the defendant company was domiciled in Spain. The applicant appealed IPEC's ruling that it had no jurisdiction to hear the action in respect of the EUTM. On appeal, the UK's Court of Appeal stayed proceedings so it could seek clarity from the CJEU regarding the interpretation of Article 97(5) of the 2009 Regulation, and it referred the following question:

> In circumstances where an undertaking is established and domiciled in Member State A and has taken steps in that territory to advertise and offer for sale goods under a sign identical to an EU trade mark on a website targeted at traders and consumers in Member State B: (i) does an EU trade mark court in Member State B have jurisdiction to hear a claim for infringement of the EU trade mark in respect of the advertisement and offer for sale of the goods in that territory?

The CJEU had regard to the intention of the legislature to provide an alternative forum thus enabling the proprietor of an EUTM to bring one or more actions, each relating specifically to the acts of infringement committed within a single EU Member State. It also considered *L'Oréal SA and Others v eBay International AG and Others*.[171] The Court viewed it apparent from the evidence submitted that the advertising and offers for sale were directed at consumers or traders situated in the UK. On this basis the applicants had a right to bring an infringement action before a court in the UK under Article 97(5) of the 2009

170 C-172/18.
171 C-324/09.

Regulation. The Court also noted that an alternative interpretation would mean that there would be no alternative jurisdiction to Article 97(1) of the 2009 Regulation, that infringers would need to do no more than ensure that its advertising and offers for sale were placed in the same jurisdiction as that where those parties are established. In response to the question raised, the CJEU confirmed that Article 97(5) should be interpreted as meaning that an EUTM court in Member State B has jurisdiction to hear an action for infringement of the EUTM in respect of the advertisement and offer for sale of the goods in that territory, provided that that advertisement and that offer specifically target the public in one or more EU Member States.

By this interpretation of the rules in Article 97(5) of the 2009 Regulation, the CJEU confirms the position for EUTM rights holders who must navigate jurisdiction of EUTM infringements online.

8. CONCLUSION

These decisions are of particular importance due to the borderless nature of the internet and the potential difficulties that arise with the ubiquitous nature of online infringement. As a result of CJEU case law, in particular the *L'Oréal* judgment, EUTM jurisdictional rules are not limited to cases where the goods in question are physically put on the market in the EU. *AMS Neve* further clarifies the position in respect of Article 125(5) of the EUTMR (Article 97(5) of the 2009 Regulation), thus providing certainty to rights holders that they can bring actions in the jurisdiction of the EU Member State which has been targeted by online offers of sales or advertising. It will be interesting to see how this jurisprudence is implemented and develops further in another 25 years' time!

IX. PROTECTING EUTMS AGAINST INFRINGEMENT THROUGH PROVISIONAL AND PROTECTIVE MEASURES

Paul MICALLEF GRIMAUD and Nikolai LUBRANO

The protection of one's Intellectual Property Rights (IPRs) through timely action is a cornerstone of IP protection, though one which invariably leads to discussion over where to file an action and what type of provisional and protective measure(s) to take. In a cross-border litigious context, this debate, and ultimately the decisions that ensue, are very often led by considerations as to which of the competent jurisdictions are more amenable to upholding the precautionary measures to be taken, the complexity of proceedings relating to the taking of such measures, the ease of enforcing such measures and the ease of cross-border enforcement of orders and measures issued by a particular court.

Regulation (EU) 2017/1001 of the European parliament and of the Council of 14 June 2017 on the European Union trade mark (**EUTMR**) has not killed this debate. If anything, it may have given rise (as it did before the Maltese Courts) to a debate as to whether the measures contemplated in the EUTMR are those that issue from Directive 2004/48/EC of 29 April 2004 on the enforcement of intellectual property rights (the "**Enforcement Directive**") or extend to any other provisional and protective measures that may be applied under national procedural laws. It is this intricate interplay of legal frameworks that gives rise to the complex analysis made by practitioners, often in a heightened state of urgency, and with one single outcome in mind – effectively protecting the client's IPRs from infringement in the most expeditious way possible.

1. JURISDICTION OVER PROVISIONAL AND PROTECTIVE MEASURES

The starting point of every cross-border litigious analysis is establishing which Court is competent and has jurisdiction to determine the matter concerned. This applies equally to the taking of provisional and protective measures.

The EUTMR is clear that there may only be one EU trade mark court ("EUTMC"), the jurisdiction of which may be established through Article 125 EUTMR. It being clear that, in accordance with Article 126 EUTMR, the EUTMC shall have exclusive jurisdiction to hear the merits of the case, Article 131(1) is equally clear that "*application may be made to the courts of a Member State, including EU trade mark courts, for such provisional, including protective, measures in respect of an EU trade mark or EU trade mark application as may be available under the law of that State in respect of a national trade mark, even if, under this Regulation, an EU trade mark court of another Member State has jurisdiction as to the substance of the matter.*"

Owing to the EUTMC not having exclusive jurisdiction to determine provisional and protective action taken by the EUTM right holder, the legal practitioner's prime consideration is whether it is more practical and effective to take such measures directly in the jurisdiction where the breach is occurring or is threatened.

It is, however, the case that no cross-border provisional and protective orders may be issued if not by the EUTMC, and subject to them being enforceable under the Brussels I *(Recast)* Regulation.[172]

2. PROVISIONAL AND PROTECTIVE MEASURES APPLICABLE TO EUTMS

As previously mentioned, a host of provisional and protective measures may be applied for to protect EUTMs from being breached. The EUTMR does not harmonise these possible measures that may be taken and instead refers to the "*measures … as may be available under the law of that State* (in which the measures are being applied for) *in respect of a national trade mark.*"[173]

172 Regulation (EU) No 1215/2012.
173 Article 131(1) EUTMR.

Despite the broad wording of this provision, debate has ensued in the Maltese Court, acting as the EUTMC, as to whether the said provision should be read to mean that any provisional and protective measures available under domestic procedural law may be applied for or whether the "*measures available under the law of that State*" are limited to those measures that are available in that Member State through the transposition of the Enforcement Directive. Moreover, seeing that the said Directive provides for a degree of harmonisation, in the event that the criteria for obtaining an injunction under the Enforcement Directive differ from the criteria to be satisfied to obtain an injunction under domestic procedural law, there is debate about whether the criteria set by the Directive are to apply to the exclusion of the criteria established under domestic procedural law.

The case in point was that of *King.com Limited (C42504) vs. Avukat Dottor Louis Cassar Pullicino noe.* (First Hall Civil Court, 18 April 2016). These proceedings were initiated by King.com, the creator of the mobile phone game "Candy Crush", which applied to the Maltese Court for a prohibitory injunction to stop a creator of similar games based in the United States from using the word "Candy" in the name of its games. "Candy" had been registered as a word mark (EUTM) in favour of the applicant.

The defendant successfully argued that, as it was dealing with an EUTM, the Maltese Court, which was acting as the EUTMC, could not apply domestic procedural law criteria for the issuing of an injunction, but ought to apply those criteria established by the CJEU and other Member State Courts in the ambit of an injunction issued under the Enforcement Directive. The focus of this argumentation was the application of the criteria of "urgency" and the "balance of prejudice" which are not failing criteria for the issuing of an injunction under Maltese procedural law. Upholding the defendant's arguments, the Court held that:

> *The fact that article 103[174] grants the applicant the right to apply for protective measures in respect of his community trademark under the laws available in the*
>
> *State where proceedings are initiated, necessarily means that once it has chosen the Maltese forum to provide the remedy requested, this Court cannot but apply the relevant procedure as laid out in council regulations and directives applicable in Malta relating to trademarks embodied in Chapter 488 of the Laws of Malta[175], to the exclusion of any other domestic law.*

174 Today, Article 113 EUTMR.

175 The Enforcement of Intellectual Property Rights (Regulation) Act, (Chapter 488 of the laws of Malta) (the "**Enforcement Act**") is that piece of Maltese legislation that transposes the Enforcement Directive into Maltese law.

Chapter 488, consequently being a transposition of the said directive into our legislation, has to be interpreted in line with the recitals to the Directive underlying its scope and application, meaning that in the granting of an injunction the Court has to keep in mind the following essential requisites:

1. proportionality of the measure;

2. guarantees needed to cover costs and injury to the respondent if the claim proves to be unjustified; and

3. irreparable harm which may be caused to the claimant by the delay in restraining the defendant from continuing in its action of infringement.

Although these requisites are not present in our national procedural laws, the Court opines that both community law as well as domestic law seem to take the stance that the granting of an injunction is an extraordinary remedy which should be resorted to with great caution. This is also in line with the scope of the CMT regulation[176] *and directives which should not undermine the free movement of goods or suppress and distort competition and which should not create barriers to legitimate trade.*

3. THE ENFORCEMENT DIRECTIVE

The Enforcement Directive is thus seen as a corollary to the EUTMR, bringing about a level of harmonisation amongst Member States in the applicability of provisional and protective measures with respect to EUTMs.

The measures listed in the Enforcement Directive are:

1. Interlocutory injunctions;
2. Seizure and delivery up of infringing goods; and
3. Seizure of bank accounts and assets of the alleged infringer, in the case of an infringement committed on a commercial scale and where it is demonstrated that eventual damages may not be recovered.

Recital 22 of the Enforcement Directive states:

> It is also essential to provide for provisional measures for the immediate termination of infringements, without awaiting a decision on the substance of the case, while observing the rights of the defence, ensuring the proportionality of the provisional measures as appropriate to the characteristics of the case in question and providing the guarantees needed to cover the costs and the injury caused to the defendant by an unjustified request. Such measures are particularly justified where any delay would cause irreparable harm to the holder of an intellectual property right.

176 The EUTMR.

Article 3 of the Enforcement Directive goes on to state:

> 1. Member States shall provide for the measures, procedures and remedies necessary to ensure the enforcement of the intellectual property rights covered by this Directive. Those measures, procedures and remedies shall be fair and equitable and shall not be unnecessarily complicated or costly, or entail unreasonable time-limits or unwarranted delays.
>
> 2. Those measures, procedures and remedies shall also be effective, proportionate and dissuasive and shall be applied in such a manner as to avoid the creation of barriers to legitimate trade and to provide for safeguards against their abuse.

In the *King.com case* it was successfully argued that, even though Article 3 of the Directive was not transposed directly into Maltese law (Chapter 488), the principle of proportionality enshrined in Article 3 of the Directive reflects the spirit of the correct application of the Directive. This would mean that, in such an instance where the court dealing with a provisional injunction application has not determined the merits of the case, or has not even begun to consider them, it should pay utmost attention not to prejudice any of the parties unnecessarily and detrimentally in the event that the merits be decided in favour of one of the parties. The court should therefore not seek to impose an injunction or other precautionary measures laid down in the Enforcement Directive, unless there is the utmost and unavoidable necessity to do so.

Moreover, the Court should weigh the prejudice that each party would suffer in the event that it upholds, or does not uphold, the request for provisional and protective measures and the case on its merits is determined in favour of one party or the other.

Another argument that was successfully made by the defendant was that Recital 22 speaks of the justification of the Court upholding a request for provisional and protective measures where *"any delay would cause irreparable harm to the holder"* of the right. The corollary of this is that there is no, or less, justification if the holder of the right does not see delay as particularly important, suggesting that there is no irreparable harm to the right holder in the instance where he fails to act expeditiously in protecting his rights by filing an application for provisional and protective measures.

The interplay between the Enforcement Directive and the EUTMR cannot therefore be understated. This notion was yet again reinforced in the same proceedings of *King.com* where, at a subsequent stage of the proceedings where the defendant obtained a stay of proceedings pending the filing of invalidity proceedings before the EUIPO, the plaintiff filed a further request for the imposition of provisional and protective measures under Article 132(3) EUTMR, which reads:

> 3. Where the EU trade mark court stays the proceedings it may order provisional and protective measures for the duration of the stay.

The plaintiff argued that, contrary to Article 131(1), the EUTMR does not speak of "*measures ... as may be available under the law of that State* (in which the measures are being applied for) *in respect of a national trade mark*" and therefore the Court's discretion as to the measures that it may apply is unfettered. The plaintiff cited the *obiter* judgment of the Düsseldorf Court in the case *Re. Anapurna*[177] in its favour. The said Court had declared that Article 132(3) "*authorises the court, which chooses to stay proceedings with regards to a case concerning the infringement of a Community trade mark on the basis of action for the invalidity of that trade mark, to order any measures which the court deems appropriate, even if those measures are not provided under the national procedural law*".

However, the Court upheld the defendant's argument that Article 132(3) should be read in conjunction with Article 131(1) and consequently, as explained above, with the Enforcement Directive, thus leading to all the above described implications. These same limitations do not necessarily arise where the domestic courts are dealing with the protection, through the application of provisional and protective measures, of purely domestic IPRs.

4. THE INTERPLAY WITH REGULATION (EU) NO 608/2013 OF THE EUROPEAN PARLIAMENT AND OF THE COUNCIL OF 12 JUNE 2013 CONCERNING CUSTOMS ENFORCEMENT OF INTELLECTUAL PROPERTY RIGHTS

EU Regulation 608/2013 sets out its own procedure affording the EUTM right holder the possibility to file an application with Customs authorities in Europe for them to take action and seize counterfeit goods detected by the said authorities. Prompt action by the Customs authorities is in fact an essential deterrent to the proliferation of counterfeit goods and Regulation 608/2013 is a powerful tool in the hands of EUTM right holders.

---

177 Düsseldorf Higher Regional Court, 19.05.2015 – I-20 U 30/14.

Regulation 608/2013 applies separately to the EUTMR, albeit the rights being exercised by the applicant derive from the fact that he is a right holder under the EUTMR. Should, in the course of the proceedings commenced through the application of Regulation 608/2013, the validity of the EUTM be challenged on the basis of which action is being taken, the focus of the litigation will shift to the EUTMR.

Being two separate, albeit linked, pieces of Community legislation, there should be nothing stopping the rights holder from applying for provisional and protective measures under the EUTMR, despite there being an application under Regulation 608/2013 in place. This may be necessary in those instances where the procedures taken under Regulation 608/2013 are being challenged and the Customs authorities are being requested to release the counterfeit goods on the grounds of a purely procedural technicality, such as the applicant not adhering to the timeframes specified in Regulation 608/2013 by the applicant.

Given the importance of Malta as a major port of entry into the EU, it is not surprising that the Maltese courts are called upon to determine such matters as mentioned above. This was the case in a recent decree issued by the First Hall of the Civil Court in "*Advocate Paul Micallef Grimaud as special mandatory of BR International Holdings Inc vs International Tobacco plc et*"[178] wherein, despite the dispute relating to a local trade mark, the defendant was requesting the immediate release of the alleged counterfeit goods because the plaintiff had failed to file the application for action within the prescribed time from the date of seizure by the Customs' authorities. In order not to run the risk of having the goods released, the plaintiff filed a precautionary warrant of description in the Courts, thus attaching the goods that were in the possession of the Customs Authorities. When this procedure was challenged by the defendant, the Court held that:

> The warrant of description is issued to protect the rights of a party. The applicants (defendants in the lawsuit on the merits) insist that the interests of the defendant (plaintiffs in the lawsuit on the merits) are already appropriately cautioned through the seizure of the goods by the Comptroller of Customs. The Court disagrees since although the right of seizure by the Comptroller of Customs emanates from the law this does not mean that the defendant should not also protect his interests since he has no control over the powers of the Comptroller and their respective rights are different although the aim is the same. The Court also considers that [...] the warrant was filed so that the defendants protect their claimed intellectual property rights and

[178] Application 98/2020 in the acts of the Warrant of Description No 47/2020 pursuant to the Sworn Application No 1287/2018 MCH.

not allow the allegedly counterfeit goods seized by the Comptroller of Customs to be released to the prejudice of the rights of the defendant as proprietor of the mark [...].

The Court does not consider that the defendant went beyond the precautionary rights that the law provides simply because another party, namely the Comptroller of Customs, took action under Chapter 414 and the EU Regulation 608/2013. The law does not prohibit or limit the defendant (plaintiff in the action on the merits) from using the ordinary legal remedies available to protect his interests [...]. These rights are not excluded because the aforementioned laws provide other specific rights (and remedies).

5. THE INTERPLAY WITH THE BRUSSELS I RECAST REGULATION

The possibility of obtaining protective and provisional orders with cross-border effect is an essential tool in the hands of the EUTM right holder. As mentioned earlier, it is only the EUTMC that may issue such orders and the Brussels I *Recast* Regulation[179] ("Brussels I") must be adhered to.[180]

Brussels I includes provisional and protective measures within the definition of "judgement", thus affording the possibility for such orders issued by a Member State Court to be enforced in all the EU Member States.

There is however a hitch. Article 2 of Brussels I does not extend the definition of "judgements" to provisional and protective orders if such measures are issued by a Court without the defendant being summoned to appear. This limitation applies unless the judgement containing the measure is served on the defendant prior to enforcement. In such a case it is only if the applicant is able to provide evidence of the servicing of the provisional and protective order on the defendant who had not been summoned to appear prior to the order being issued, that the same order may be recognised and enforced in a Member State other than that whose Court issued the order.

This often creates a significant hurdle for the applicant who, needing to act swiftly to protect his rights, asks for Court protection through the issuing of provisional and protective measures unbeknownst to the defendant. The element of surprise is often crucial to ensure that the orders are effectively enforced. The requirement to notify the defendant prior to the enforcement of such orders hinders the efficacy of such orders. This applies most evidently to orders for the

179 Regulation (EU) No 1215/2012 on jurisdiction and the recognition and enforcement of judgments in civil and commercial matters (*Recast*).

180 Article 131(2) EUTMR.

seizure of the defendant's bank accounts or the contravening goods, considered in Article 9(1)(b) and 9(2) of the Enforcement Directive.

The Enforcement Directive attempts to do away with such a situation, providing specifically that:

> Member States shall ensure that the provisional measures referred to in paragraphs 1 and 2 may, in appropriate cases, be taken without the defendant having been heard, in particular where any delay would cause irreparable harm to the rightsholder. In that event, the parties shall be so informed without delay after the execution of the measures at the latest.[181]

Yet, the discrepancy between Brussels I and the Enforcement Directive remains to be resolved.

6. CONCLUSION

This short snapshot of the intricacies underlying the taking of provisional and protective measures goes to show that the various laws that come into play in this area may lead to some pitfalls and a level of lack of harmonisation in the approaches taken by different Member State courts, which, together with the CJEU, are bound to continue to shape the map leading EUTM right holders to their desired destination – effective protection against abuse.

181 Article 9(4) of the Enforcement Directive.

X. BREXIT: EQUIVALENT RIGHTS AND CONTINUED INFLUENCE OF CJEU CASE LAW

Matthew HARRIS

1. THE BASIC BREXIT LEGISLATIVE FRAMEWORK

The European Union (Withdrawal) Act 2018 (the 'Withdrawal Act') received royal assent on 26 June 2018, almost one year after it had been introduced before the UK Parliament as the Great Repeal Bill.

The Withdrawal Act stipulated that on 'exit day', the European Communities Act 1972 would be repealed. As the European Communities Act 1972 provided the domestic legislative foundation for European Community law in the United Kingdom (UK), any European law that had not already been domestically implemented by exit day would no longer form part of UK law from that date. The Withdrawal Act also provided for the incorporation into domestic law on exit day of all direct EU legislation existing at that date.

'Exit day' was initially set as 11:00 pm on 29 March 2019 but was postponed on three occasions pursuant to Article 50(3) of the Treaty on European Union; ultimately until 11:00 pm on 31 January 2020.[182]

In late 2019 the terms of the UK's withdrawal from the European Union (the 'Withdrawal Agreement') were agreed.[183] As a consequence, changes were made to the Withdrawal Act[184] providing in large part for the continuation of the operation of European Union (EU) law following exit day for an 'implementation

182 The European Union (Withdrawal) Act 2018 (Exit Day) (Amendment) Regulations 2019 (S.I. 2019 No. 718), The European Union (Withdrawal) Act 2018 (Exit Day) (Amendment) (No. 2) Regulations 2019 (S.I. 2019 No. 859) and The European Union (Withdrawal) Act 2018 (Exit Day) (Amendment) (No. 3) Regulations 2019 (S.I. 2019 No. 1423).

183 2019/C 384 I/01. The terms of the Withdrawal Agreement were agreed between the parties on 17 October 2019, with the Withdrawal Agreement entering into force on 1 February 2020.

184 By the European Union (Withdrawal Agreement) Act 2020.

period' ending at 11pm on 31 December 2020. This date was designated as 'IP Completion Day'.[185] The Withdrawal Agreement was also given direct effect as a matter of UK law.[186]

In December 2020 the UK-EU Trade and Cooperation Agreement (the 'Cooperation Agreement') was also agreed. The Cooperation Agreement contains a large number of provisions relating to intellectual property.[187]

So far as trade marks are concerned[188], the Cooperation Agreement essentially binds the parties to certain minimum provisions of trade mark law that are already part of EU and UK law and does not substantively change that law. As such, the Cooperation Agreement limits the parties' ability to develop trade mark law in a divergent manner. For example, there is no requirement that UK trade mark law should continue to protect trade marks with a reputation in the UK from use without due cause that takes unfair advantage of, or is detrimental to, the distinctive character or the repute of the trade mark.[189] In contrast, there is a requirement that the law provides for the seizure of counterfeit goods in transit.[190]

Articles 258 to 267 of the Cooperation Agreement also closely mirror some of the provisions of the EU Enforcement Directive 2004/48/EC. This is perhaps unsurprising since the UK government had previously taken the stance that the provisions of the Enforcement Directive, although representing EU best practice, were in large part derived from UK law.[191]

The Cooperation Agreement was given effect in UK law by the European Union (Future Relationship) Act 2020. The Future Relationship Act allowed for the making of secondary legislation and regulations to implement the Cooperation

185 Somewhat confusingly for intellectual property professionals, IP in this context stands for 'implementation period' and not for 'intellectual property'.

186 By Section 7A of the Withdrawal Act (introduced by section 5 of the European Union (Withdrawal Agreement) Act 2020.

187 Arts. 219 to 275.

188 Arts. 236 to 244.

189 As currently to be found, for example, in art. 9(2)(c) of the EU Trade Mark Regulation 2017/1001 and s.10(3) of the Trade Marks Act 1994.

190 See arts. 238(2) and (3) of the Cooperation Agreement mirroring art.9(4) of the EU Trade Mark Regulation 2017/1001 and s.10A of the Trade Marks Act 1994.

191 See for example the Final Regulatory Impact Assessment attached to the Explanatory Memorandum to The Intellectual Property (Enforcement, etc.) Regulations 2006 (S.I. 2006 No. 1028) prepared by the UK Department of Trade and Industry. For a more detailed examination of the implementation and operation of the Enforcement Directive in the UK and in particular England, see M. Harris, 'Enforcement of Intellectual Property Rights in the United Kingdom' in F. Petillion (ed.) *Enforcement of Intellectual Property Rights in the EU Member States*, Antwerp, Intersentia, 2019 p.1161 to 1230.

Agreement[192], but section 29 also declared that UK domestic law would have effect:

> with such modifications as are required for the purposes of implementing in that law the Trade and Cooperation Agreement ... so far as the agreement concerned is not otherwise so implemented and so far as such implementation is necessary for the purposes of complying with the international obligations of the United Kingdom under the agreement.

The vague nature of this section has been the subject of criticism and controversy, but it remains to be seen to what extent this will have any practical effect so far as the intellectual property provisions of the Cooperation Agreement are concerned. Of particular interest will be how the courts will approach the non-discrimination, 'national treatment' rules set out in Article 224, and the impact of Articles 258 to 267, which arguably mean that aspects of the EU Enforcement Directive now have direct effect.

2. THE CREATION IN THE UNITED KINGDOM OF THE COMPARABLE TRADE MARK (EU)

The EU Trade Marks Directive 89/104/EEC was implemented in the UK by the Trade Marks Act 1994. The UK government also implemented, with effect from 14 January 2019, all the changes mandated by the EU Trade Marks Directive (EU) 2015/2436.[193] Accordingly, Brexit required no fundamental changes to national trade mark law.

The position in relation to EU registered trade marks was obviously very different. The EU Trade Mark Regulation (EU) 2017/1001 (EUTMR) (as was also the case with the Community Design Regulation (EC) No 6/2002) could not continue to directly operate in the UK where the UK was no longer part of the EU institutions. Therefore, something more was required than the general saving mechanism provided by the Withdrawal Act.

The Withdrawal Agreement contained extensive provisions regarding intellectual property in general, and EU trade marks in particular.[194] However, the UK government decided to unilaterally implement much of what appeared in the Withdrawal Agreement by way of a series of statutory instruments, which were intended to have effect regardless of whether a withdrawal agreement could be concluded.

192 S. 31 of the European Union (Future Relationship) Act 2020.
193 By The Trade Marks Regulations 2018 (S.I. 2018 No. 825).
194 Art. 54 to 59.

In the case of trade marks, the key provisions were and are to be found in The Trade Marks (Amendments etc.) (EU Exit) Regulations 2019 No. 269 (SI 2019/269) and the Designs and International Trade Marks (Amendment etc.) (EU Exit) Regulations 2019 No. 638 (SI 2019/638) as amended.[195]

SI 2019/269 provided that, subject to a voluntary opt-out mechanism, all EU trade marks (including collective and certification marks) automatically converted on IP Completion Day into what is described as a 'comparable trade mark (EU)'. The comparable trade marks are deemed to have been filed on the filing date of the EU trade marks from which they derive (and to benefit from the same claims of priority and seniority as those EU trade marks) and, subject to subsequent renewal in the UK[196], expire at the same time as would have been the case with the corresponding EU trade mark.

Essentially, these comparable trade marks are then treated in the same manner as ordinary UK trade marks, subject to the following modifications.

1. If and when the comparable trade mark (EU) is challenged on the grounds of five years of non-use (whether that be when the mark is relied upon as a prior right in opposition or invalidity proceedings, by way of a defence in infringement proceedings, or in revocation proceedings), the trade mark owner can rely upon use, anywhere in the EU, of the corresponding EU trade mark during any part of the relevant 5 year period that pre-dates IP Completion Day.[197]
2. Should any issue of reputation of the comparable trade mark (EU) prior to the IP Completion Day arise, then it is the reputation of the corresponding EU trade mark across the EU that is considered.

Provision was also made in the relevant regulations in respect of the continuation of licences, the registration of security interests, and the interpretation of pre-existing agreements, documents and consents that refer to EU trade marks.

SI 2019/638 also put in place equivalent provisions in the case of international registrations designating the European Union, creating a 'comparable trade mark (IR)'.

---

195 The Intellectual Property (Amendment etc.) (EU Exit) Regulations 2020 (S.I. 2020 No. 1050) amended a number of errors in the intellectual property statutory instruments already made, and also replaced the words 'exit day' used in those statutory instruments with 'IP completion day'.

196 Specific procedures being put in place for those comparable trade marks that would expire within 6 months of IP Completion Day. See para. 5 of sch. 2A to the Trade Marks Act 1994 as inserted by SI 2019/269.

197 Para. 7 to 9 of sch. 2A of the Trade Marks Act, inserted by SI 2019/269.

3. CONTINUING INTERACTION BETWEEN EU TRADE MARKS AND COMPARABLE TRADE MARKS (EU)

The creation of the comparable trade mark (EU) was limited to EU trade marks registered on IP Completion Day. In the case of any EU trade mark application made prior to IP Completion Day that had yet to proceed to grant, trade mark owners were granted the option to apply for a UK trade mark that would benefit from the filing and priority date of the EU trade mark. However, the ability to make such an application came to an end on 30 September 2021.[198]

If an EU trade mark was subject to revocation or invalidity proceedings on IP Completion Day then, insofar as that mark is subsequently revoked or invalidated, the general rule is that the comparable trade mark (EU) will also be revoked or invalidated.[199] There is, however, an exception to the general rule[200] where the grounds for revocation or invalidity would not apply to the comparable trade mark (EU) had it existed at the date the cancellation proceedings were instituted. For example, if the ground for revocation of the EU trade mark was a prior right in a member state other than the UK, then the comparable trade mark (EU) would not be revoked.

The question has also arisen as to how the UK Intellectual Property Office (UKIPO) should deal with applications for UK trade marks that were subject to ongoing oppositions and invalidity actions based upon EU trade marks on IP Completion Day. Although the relevant EU trade marks were likely on IP Completion Day to have led to the creation of a comparable trade mark (EU), the approach of the UKIPO has been to determine these proceedings by reference to the law and marks (including EU trade marks) that existed at the date the proceedings commenced. Not only is this the approach mandated by SI 2019/269[201] but it is consistent with the principle of continuity of law.[202]

This is in contrast with the approach of the EU Intellectual Property Office (EUIPO), which has taken the position that UK prior rights would be disregarded

198 Para. 25 Ibid.

199 Para. 21A of sch. 2A of the Trade Marks Act, inserted by para. 9 of Pt. 4 of The Intellectual Property (Amendment etc.) (EU Exit) Regulations 2020 (S.I. 2020 No. 1050).

200 Provided by para. 21A (4) Ibid.

201 Reg. 4 of SI 2019/269 removed EU trade marks from the list of prior rights that might be relied upon in such an opposition, but para. 7 of sch. 5 to SI 2019/269 states that any pre-existing applications and proceedings should be dealt with under the old law.

202 See the detailed discussion of transitional provisions and continuity of the law in *Bentley Motors Limited v (1) Bentley 1962 Limited (2) Brandlogic Limited* [2020] EWCA Civ 1726 (16 December 2020) paras. 55 to 60.

when it came to proceedings before it, even if the relevant proceedings had commenced prior to IP Completion Day.[203]

There existed a possibility, therefore, that UK trade mark applications could be denied (or that UK trade marks could be invalidated) on the basis of earlier EU trade marks that, on a proper analysis prior to IP Completion Day, are themselves invalid.

Changes were made to the law in late 2021 in order to address the perceived unfairness of this result.[204] In cases where UK trade mark opposition or invalidity proceedings commenced prior to IP Completion Day and the application or mark is challenged on the basis of an EU trade mark, the applicant or proprietor can counter-challenge the comparable trade mark (EU) that corresponds to the relevant EU trade mark. If the comparable trade mark (EU) is then found to be invalid or revoked, the EU trade mark can no longer be relied upon in the opposition or invalidity proceedings.

4. THE STATUS OF THE CJEU AND CJEU CASE LAW POST BREXIT

Although cases already referred to the Court of Justice of the European Union (CJEU) prior to IP Completion Day could proceed to a decision[205], on that date the power of the UK courts to make further references to the CJEU fell away.[206]

The decisions of the CJEU prior to IP Completion Day on issues of retained EU law constitute 'retained EU case law' that continue to be binding on all UK

---

203 Paras.11 and 12 of Communication No. 2/20 of the Executive Director of the Office of 10 September 2020. See, for example, the decision of the Opposition Division No B 3 029 595. The legality of the approach of the CJEU is questionable. The General Court considered this in its decision of 6 October 2021, *Indo European Foods v EUIPO – Chakari (Abresham Super Basmati Selaa Grade One World's Best Rice)*, T-342/20, ECLI:EU:T:2021:651, but on the particular facts of the case did not need to decide the issue. However, as the EUIPO observed in *Basmati*, where an EU trade mark application is successfully opposed on the basis of UK rights only, the applicant would still be able to convert the application into national trade mark applications in all remaining Member States.

204 The Trade Marks and International Trade Marks (Amendment) (EU Exit) Regulations 2021 (S.I. 2021 No. 1235), which came into force on 26 November 2021.

205 The CJEU's continued competence in this respect was confirmed by Art.86 (2) of the Withdrawal Agreement. However, on IP Completion Day, there were no extant IP related referrals from the UK courts to the CJEU. The last reference of the UK courts to the CJEU in an IP case was in late 2019 in C-728/19 *Beverly Hills Teddy Bear v PMS International Group PLC*, which involved questions of European unregistered design law. The matter was settled prior to determination by the CJEU.

206 S. 6(1)(b) of the European Union (Withdrawal) Act 2018.

courts subject to a number of limited exceptions.[207] Those binding decisions would appear to encompass the decisions of the General Court.[208]

Initially, only the UK Supreme Court (and in limited cases the High Court of Justiciary in Scotland) had the right to depart from decisions of the CJEU.[209] More recently that power was also granted to a number of additional appeal courts[210], the most significant of which for intellectual property purposes is the English Court of Appeal.

Under the relevant regulations, when deciding whether to depart from a CJEU decision, the relevant court must apply the test that the Supreme Court would apply when deciding whether to depart from its own case law.[211]

That test is 'when it appears right to do so'.[212] Although that phrase might suggest a wide discretion, in practice the Supreme Court has exercised its power to depart somewhat sparingly. The Supreme Court has had regard not just to whether it considers any previous decision to be wrong, but also whether the principle is long standing, the principle has been relied upon in many cases, and to what extent amendment to the law had already been considered and addressed by parliament.[213]

There are a significant number of previous decisions of the CJEU on questions of trade mark law that the English courts have expressed dissatisfaction with, and which might be said to provide obvious candidates for departure.

---

207 S. 6(3) and 6(7) of the European Union (Withdrawal) Act 2018.

208 According to s. 21 of the European Union (Withdrawal) Act 2018 'European Court' is given the meaning to be found in sch. 1 of the Interpretation Act 1978. This defined the 'European Court' as 'the Court of Justice of the European Union'. In *Jaguar Land Rover Ltd v Bombardier Recreational Products Inc* [2016] EWHC B37 the English High Court held that the English courts were bound by decisions of the General Court because (a) sch.1 to the European Communities Act 1972 also defined the 'European Court' as the Court of Justice of the European Union, and (b) art.19(1) of the Treaty on European Union provides that: 'The Court of Justice of the European Union shall include the Court of Justice, the General Court and specialised courts.' Although the European Communities Act 1972 has now been repealed, this reasoning would appear to be equally applicable to the identical definition of European Court to be found in sch. 1 of the Interpretation Act 1978.

209 S. 6(4) European Union (Withdrawal) Act 2018.

210 The European Union (Withdrawal) Act 2018 (Relevant Court) (Retained EU Case Law) Regulations 2020 (S.I. 2020 No. 1525).

211 S. 6(5) European Union (Withdrawal) Act 2018 and Reg. 5 of SI 2020/1525.

212 Recorded in the House of Lords Practice Statement of 26 July 1966 and which was reaffirmed to be applicable to the Supreme Court in *Austin v Mayor and Burgesses of the London Borough of Southwark* [2010] UKSC 28 at para. 25.

213 See para. 25 to 27 *supra*.

They include, for example, *L'Oreal SA v Bellure NV*[214], in which Lord Justice Jacob did 'not agree with or welcome' the conclusions of the CJEU in respect of comparative advertising and trade mark infringement in that case but his 'duty' was to apply them.[215] However, as yet there does not appear to have been a trade mark case in which any English court has been invited to depart from European case law.

The recent decision of the English Court of Appeal in *Tunein Inc v Warner Music UK Ltd & Anor*[216] is also not encouraging for those hoping for a radical change in the law. In this case, the Court of Appeal was invited by one of the parties to depart from CJEU case law on retained EU copyright law as to the meaning of 'communication to the public'. The Court of Appeal declined to do so, notwithstanding that the Advocate General had also recently suggested that a different approach might be appropriate.[217] In reaching its decision, the Court of Appeal recognised that CJEU case law on the subject was not free of difficulty or criticism but decided to follow it, particularly where it was unconvinced that a better solution was readily available. It also remarked upon what it characterised as the CJEU's 'unrivalled experience' in addressing this area of the law.

So far as decisions of the CJEU after IP Completion Day are concerned, the basic legal position is different. The UK courts are not bound by any decision of the CJEU made after Brexit, but 'may have regard to anything done on or after exit day by the European Court'.[218] What 'having regard to' means in practice has been the subject of considerable debate. However, the English courts (and in particular the higher English courts) have frequently considered and taken account of the decisions of (i) courts in other common law states when considering questions of common law and (ii) the decisions of the courts of other Member States on questions of European law, despite not being bound by them. Therefore, CJEU decisions are likely to continue to be highly influential on questions of retained EU law unless and until the UK legislature diverges from that law.

The *Tunein Inc* case is again of interest in this respect because the Court of Appeal not only took into account but followed CJEU caselaw post-dating IP Completion Day on the issue of 'communication to the public'.

214 *L'Oreal SA & Ors v Bellure NV & Ors* [2010] EWCA Civ 535 (21 May 2010).
215 *Ibid.*, para. 50.
216 *Tunein Inc v Warner Music UK Ltd & Anor* [2021] EWCA Civ 441 (26 March 2021).
217 In particular the opinion of Advocate General Szpunar of 10 September 2020, *VG Bild-Kunst v Stiftung Preußischer Kulturbesitz, C-392/19,* ECLI:EU:C:2020:696.
218 See s. 6(2) of the European Union (Withdrawal) Act 2018.

5. PRE-EXISTING EU TRADE MARK LITIGATION IN THE UK COURTS POST BREXIT

Paragraph 20 of the new Schedule 2A to the Trade Marks Act 1994, inserted by Schedule 1 of SI 2019/269, provides that where an existing EU trade mark was the subject of proceedings still pending in the UK courts on IP Completion Day[219], the UK courts could still proceed to determine that litigation and that (subject to a number of exclusions)[220] Chapter 10 of the EUTMR (which gave jurisdiction to the relevant UK courts to determine EU trade mark actions) would still apply. That right was confirmed using slightly different wording in the Withdrawal Agreement.[221]

SI 2019/269 also provided that where a UK court was dealing with an EU infringement action, it had the power to grant an injunction prohibiting the unauthorised use of the comparative trade mark (EU). This clearly makes sense given that following IP Completion Day, EU trade marks ceased to be of legal effect in the UK and only injunctive relief in respect of the comparative trade mark (EU) would safeguard against ongoing infringement in the UK.

The Explanatory Memorandum to the 2019 Regulation and (at least initially) guidance published by the UKIPO suggested that the remedies that might be granted by a UK court would be limited to the comparable trade mark (EU).[222] That memorandum and guidance appears to have been wrong as a matter of UK law even prior to the Withdrawal Agreement. The reason for this is that the power of the UK court to grant an injunction prohibiting the unauthorised use of the comparative trade mark (EU) was expressed to be 'without prejudice to any other relief by way of damages, accounts or otherwise available to the proprietor of the existing EUTM'.[223] So, for example, the UK court appeared to retain the

219 Strictly this is limited to proceedings in UK courts previously designated as an EU trade mark court under art.123 of the EUTMR. However, in England this covers the High Court (including the Intellectual Property Enterprise Court) and a number of County Courts – see Reg. 12 of the Community Trade Mark Regulations 2006 (S.I. 2006 No. 1027) as amended by The European Union Trade Mark Regulations 2016 (S.I. 2016 No. 299) and the Trade Mark Regulations 2018 (S.I. 2018 No. 825).

220 The exceptions being art. 128(2), (4), (6) and (7) and 132 of the EUTMR governing related actions. Whether those exceptions are consistent with the Withdrawal Agreement was called into question in *Easygroup Ltd v Beauty Perfectionists Ltd & Ors* [2021] EWHC 3385 (Ch) (17 December 2021), but the court did not need to decide the issue (see paragraph 54 of the judgment).

221 Art. 67 1.(b).

222 The relevant wording of the Explanatory Memorandum is at paragraph 7.15. The Guidance published by the UK IPO as updated on 3 December 2020 is recorded on the Internet Archive at www.web.archive.org/web/20201220070142/https://www.gov.uk/guidance/eu-trademark-protection-and-comparable-uk-trademarks.

223 Para. 20(3) of sch. 2A to the Trade Marks Act 1994 inserted by SI 2019/269.

right under UK law to grant a pan-European injunction under Article 130 of the EUTMR, which paragraph 20 of the new Schedule 2A to the Trade Marks Act 1994 stated continued to apply.

In any event, following the Withdrawal Agreement, the ability of the UK courts to grant pan-European injunctions appears to have been a clear and firm foundation in EU law, which in turn is of direct effect in UK law. Further, the contention that no such right remained in UK law was recently rejected by the English High Court in *Easygroup Ltd v Beauty Perfectionists Ltd & Ors [2021] EWHC 3385* (Ch) (17 December 2021).[224]

6. NEW EU TRADE MARK LITIGATION IN THE UK COURTS POST BREXIT

Currently, it takes approximately 12 to 15 months for an English trade mark action to come to trial. Exactly how many cases involving EU trade marks were pending on IP Completion Day, and which remain unresolved whether through the courts or otherwise, is unclear. However, the transitional provisions in both SI 2019/269 and the Withdrawal Agreement in respect of such proceedings will be of diminishing practical importance as these cases are resolved.

So far as proceedings commenced after IP Completion Day are concerned, no UK court remains an EU trade mark court entitled as such to deal with EU trade mark infringement actions. However, it does not necessarily follow that the UK courts, and the English courts in particular, will not in future be prepared to hear EU trade mark infringement claims.

Historically, the English courts had been reluctant to hear actions for infringement of foreign intellectual property rights. There were a number of overlapping reasons given for this. The first was by extension to intellectual property cases of a principle, known as the '*Moçambique* rule'[225], that an English court had no jurisdiction to entertain an action for the determination of the title to, or the right to possession of, foreign land, or the recovery of damages for trespass to such land. The second was that under the general rule of torts, often identified as 'the rule in *Phillips v Eyre*'[226], an act done in

224 The judge granted leave to appeal that decision, although at the time this article was being completed (in mid-January 2022), it was unclear whether such an appeal is being pursued.

225 Named after the nineteenth century House of Lords decision in *British South Africa Co v Companhia de Moçambique* [1893] AC 602.

226 See comments at para. 62 of *Lucasfilm Ltd & Ors v Ainsworth & Anor* [2011] UKSC 39.

a foreign country is a tort if it is both (1) wrongful according to the law of the country where it was done, and, (2) wrongful according to English law (i.e. is an act which, if done in England, would be a tort). As infringement of a foreign intellectual property right was not unlawful in England, it would not (so the argument went) satisfy that test. The third was that, in the case of rights created by the exercise of the sovereign power of the state (whether that be rights in land or intellectual property), comity of nations required that only the relevant state should decide any controversy in relation to that property. This was also described as the act of state doctrine, whereby the court of one country would not sit in judgment on the acts of the government of another done within its territory. For an English court to question the validity of a foreign intellectual property right, particularly if it was a registered right, would, it was argued, offend against that principle.

However, the *Moçambique* rule was abolished in cases of immovable property by section 30(1) of the Civil Jurisdiction and Judgments Act 1982. The rule in *Phillips v Eyre* was eroded in a number of subsequent cases and abolished so far as intellectual property cases are concerned by section 10 of the Private International Law (Miscellaneous Provisions) Act 1995. That left the doctrine of act of state.

This issue then came before the UK Supreme Court in 2011 in *Lucasfilm Ltd & Ors v Ainsworth & Anor.*[227] In that case, proceedings were brought against an individual and a company based in England in respect of the sale on the internet, into the US, of replica copies of Stormtrooper helmets (made famous by the Star Wars franchise). The English Court of Appeal refused to allow enforcement of a US court judgement in respect of those activities and the Supreme Court went on to consider whether it was possible to bring proceedings in England for infringement of US copyrights.

Having reviewed the relevant legislation and previous cases, the Supreme Court held that this would be possible. The way the case was argued meant that the court did not need to express an opinion on the issue of litigating other foreign intellectual property rights. One of the judges in that case was also at pains to make clear that he had expressed no view about the application or scope of the doctrine of act of state in relation to issues of validity of foreign intellectual property rights which (unlike copyright) may be said to depend upon state grant.[228]

---

227 *Lucasfilm Ltd & Ors v Ainsworth & Anor* [2011] UKSC 39.
228 See the comments of Lord Mance at para. 115.

Nevertheless, in its reasoning the court held that the doctrine of act of state did not preclude an action for infringement of foreign intellectual property rights, even if the validity of those rights was in issue, simply because the action calls into question the decision of a foreign official. This decision, therefore, strongly suggests that, provided that an entity is subject to the jurisdiction of the English courts (for example by reason of its domicile), those courts could as a matter of English law determine a question of foreign infringement of a registered intellectual property right. This is particularly so if no issue of validity is raised. Neither SI 2019/269 nor the Withdrawal Agreement expressly state that EU trade marks should be treated differently.

Such an outcome is arguably consistent with the historic EU approach. Not only was this the pre-Brexit position under the EUTMR but the CJEU has held that under the Brussels Regulation European courts can determine issues of patent infringement in other states unless and until validity is challenged.[229] The Supreme Court in *Lucasfilm* also examined, and appears to have been influenced by, the European approach.[230]

The Brussels Regulation is no longer in force in the UK, having been expressly repealed in the UK on IP Completion Day.[231] The UK has applied to join the Lugano Convention, but to date the EU Commission has been obstructive in this respect.[232] Nevertheless, the *Lucasfilm* decision suggests that, quite separate from the provisions of the Brussels Regulation and the Lugano Convention, proceedings for infringement of EU intellectual property rights in the English Courts are still permitted under the English common law.

However, one significant consequence of the repeal of the Brussels Regulation, and the lack of any like-for-like replacement, is that the English courts are no longer bound by either the mandatory provisions of the Brussels Regulation or the Lugano Convention. Consequently, the old English rules of *forum non conveniens* now also apply. In other words, even if the English courts can consider a claim of EU trade mark infringement, they may in particular circumstances decline to do so.

---

229 Judgment of the CJEU of 13 July 2006, *Gesellschaft für Antriebstechnik mbH & Co KG (GAT) v Lamellen und Kupplungsbau Beteiligungs KG (LuK)*, C-4/03, ECLI:EU:C:2006:457.

230 Paras. 88 to 93.

231 Civil Jurisdiction and Judgments (Amendment) (EU Exit) Regulations 2019 (S.I. 2019 No.479) (Exit Regulations), as amended by the Civil, Criminal and Family Justice (Amendment) (EU Exit) Regulations 2020 (S.I. 2020 No. 1493).

232 See the Note Verbale communication of the European Commission to the Swiss Federal Council as the Depository of the 2007 Lugano Convention, a copy of which is available at www.eda.admin.ch/dam/eda/fr/documents/aussenpolitik/voelkerrecht/autres-conventions/Lugano2/20210701-LUG-ann-EU.pdf.

The fact that an English court might be prepared to determine an infringement action in respect of EU intellectual property rights also does not mean that any such finding would be respected by another European court. A basic difficulty is that Article 125 of the EUTMR does not allow for determination of European trade mark infringement actions other than in an EU trade mark court. The EUIPO has already expressly stated that the English courts no longer have competence in this area and that '[d]isputes on the infringement and the validity of EU trade marks involving EU trade mark owners established in the UK must be settled by EU trade mark courts'.[233]

7. EXHAUSTION AFTER BREXIT

Prior to the adoption of the doctrine of exhaustion into UK law, the English courts historically applied a concept of implied consent in respect of the sale of goods. This provided that, absent express provision to the contrary, a purchaser of goods had a right to subsequently freely deal in those purchased goods (including by way of export or import) notwithstanding the seller's intellectual property rights.

The doctrine of implied consent had originated in patent cases but was also applied to trade mark cases.[234] Consent to subsequent sale of goods by the purchaser could also be implied where the entity selling the products in one market, whilst being a separate legal entity to that which owned the relevant UK rights, formed part of the same group.[235]

However, since the doctrine of implied consent was dependent upon the deemed consent of the rightsholder, there could be circumstances where the court considered it inappropriate to imply consent. So, for example, in *Colgate-Palmolive Ltd v Markwell Finance Ltd*[236] the Court of Appeal rejected an implied consent argument where genuine but inferior quality toothpaste, originally sold in Brazil, had been parallel imported into the UK.

---

233 See the answer to question 6 of the EU IPO guidance as to the 'General impact on EUTMs and RCSs' available at www.euipo.europa.eu/ohimportal/lt/law/brexit-q-and-a/general-impact-on-ip-rights.

234 Attempts to apply it in cases involving copyright have been less successful, at least in modern times. See in this respect *Polydor Ltd. v. Harlequin Record Shop* [1980] F.S.R. 362.

235 *Revlon Inc. v. Cripps & Lee Ltd.* [1980] F.S.R. 85.

236 *Colgate-Palmolive Ltd v Markwell Finance Ltd* [1989] RPC 497.

Following the *Silhouette*[237] and *Zino Davidoff*[238] decisions, the separate doctrine of exhaustion effectively superseded and displaced the doctrine of implied consent in the UK, so far as trade mark law was concerned, in circumstances where goods were imported from outside of the EU. Not only did exhaustion apply within the EU but Member States were also precluded from adopting a doctrine of international exhaustion. As such, for consent to provide a defence where products were imported from outside of the EU, that consent had to be 'unequivocally demonstrated'.

With Brexit, and with the intellectual property rights in goods first placed on the market in the UK no longer being exhausted in the EU, the following question arose: what would happen to the doctrine of exhaustion following Brexit? A particularly pressing concern here for the UK government appears to have been the parallel trade in pharmaceuticals imported for use by the National Health Service. Such imports were estimated in 2019 to save the service £100 million per annum.[239]

The Intellectual Property (Exhaustion of Rights) (EU Exit) Regulations 2019 No 265 (SI 2019/265), made prior to both the Withdrawal Agreement and the Cooperation Agreement, provided at least an initial answer to that question. SI 2019/265 amended the relevant intellectual property legislation so that after 1 January 2021, intellectual property rights continued to be exhausted in the UK by the placing of goods on the market in the European Economic Area with the rights holder's consent.

The issue of exhaustion was then addressed in Article 223 of the Cooperation Agreement, which stated that the intellectual property provisions of the Cooperation Agreement, '[do] not affect the freedom of the parties to determine whether and under what conditions the exhaustion of intellectual property rights applies'.

It was with this freedom in mind that the issue of exhaustion of rights was recently subject to a UK governmental consultation.[240] This consultation

237 Judgment of the CJEU of 16 July 1998, *Silhouette International Schmied GmbH & Co. KG v Hartlauer Handelsgesellschaft mbH*, C-355/96, ECLI:EU:C:1998:374.

238 Judgment of the CJEU of 20 November 2001, *Zino Davidoff SA v A&G Imports Ltd*, C-414/99 to C-416/99, ECLI:EU:C:2001:617.

239 According to an Ernst & Young study on the Exhaustion of Intellectual Property Rights commissioned by the UK Intellectual Property Office and published in June 2019 (see s. 5.2 of that study) available at www.assets.publishing.service.gov.uk/government/uploads/system/uploads/attachment_data/file/808871/Exhaustion-of-intellectual-property-rights.pdf.

240 Published on 7 June 2021 by the UKIPO and which ran from then until 31 August 2021.

sought views on the future of the exhaustion regime in the UK, including (i) whether different rights and products might justify different exhaustion regimes and (ii) seeking views as to whether it would be preferable in the UK to have a full international exhaustion regime, a national exhaustion regime or the continuance of the present UK plus European Economic Area (referred to as 'UK+') approach.

Significantly, the UK government expressed the view in its consultation paper that bringing in a national exhaustion regime, whereby intellectual property rights could be used to stop goods that originate in the European Economic Area from being imported into Northern Ireland, would be incompatible with the Northern Ireland Protocol.[241] Whether this view is correct has been the subject of much debate.[242] It is also in marked contrast with the European Commission's view that intellectual property rights are not exhausted in the EU where goods are first legally placed on the market in Northern Ireland.[243]

The CJEU continues to have jurisdiction to deal with certain issues under the Northern Ireland Protocol.[244] This raises the possibility that, should a national exhaustion regime be adopted across the UK, the question of its compatibility with the Protocol could come before the CJEU. However, it seems unlikely that the UK government will adopt national exhaustion at any time soon, particularly given the initial views of the UK government on this issue as expressed in the consultation paper, the fact that certain elements of the governing Conservative party favour more rather than less exhaustion[245], and the political sensitivity of the UK government on issues of CJEU competence. It remains to be seen whether these issues come before the CJEU as a result of a reference in intellectual property proceedings from the Irish courts.

---

241 See the section 'Interaction with Northern Ireland Protocol' at pg. 11 of the Consultation document and available at www.gov.uk/government/consultations/uks-future-exhaustion-of-intellectual-property- rights-regime.

242 See for example the submission of the United Kingdom's Intellectual Property Lawyer's Association in response to the consultation and available on its website at www.ipla.org.uk/submissions.

243 See Notice to Stakeholders dated 25 June 2020, footnote 9 available at www.ec.europa.eu/info/sites/default/files/brexit_files/info_site/exhaustion-ip-rights_en.pdf.

244 Although at the time of writing the UK government were seeking that these powers of the CJEU be removed.

245 See paras. 512 to 516 of the report of the Taskforce on Innovation, Growth and Regulatory Reform available at www.gov.uk/government/publications/taskforce-on-innovation-growth-and-regulatory-reform-independent-report.

www.ingramcontent.com/pod-product-compliance
Ingram Content Group UK Ltd.
Pitfield, Milton Keynes, MK11 3LW, UK
UKHW051923100926
8556IPUK00021B/1334

9 781839 702440